True Life Stories Dictated by Former American Slaves in the 1930's

Book 1:
DESCRIPTIONS OF
PLANTATION LIFE

Compiled by

Donna Wyant Howell

Cover Photograph:

Old Goose Creek Plantation
Charleston, SC

AMERICAN LEGACY™ Books • Washington, DC

The **I WAS A SLAVE**™ Book Collection

AMERICAN LEGACY™ **Books**

Library of Congress Catalog Card Number: 98-73931

ISBN 1-886766-08-8

Published in the U.S.A.
Publisher:
American Legacy Books
Washington, DC

Revised first edition, first printing, 1998
(First edition, 1995)

Contents

The **I WAS A SLAVE** Book Collection
is dedicated to the millions* of enslaved people
whose toil helped to create America

Cora Wyant and her children

and to my great-grandmother
CORA WYANT
1856-1963
who first stirred my interest when I was nine
by telling me about that wonderful day when she was nine
when she and her mother held hands
as they walked off the plantation
— FREE!

and to all the descendents of African slaves,
as well as African American freeborns
(including my maternal freeborn ancestors)
who suffered indirectly due to the institution of slavery

and to the millions of my brothers and sisters
who today still bear much weight.

(*estimated total transported from Africa and born into slavery: over 60 million
from 1565 to 1865)

4

Important Information

This book is one in the series of The I WAS A SLAVE™ Book Collection. It contains excerpts and full interviews revealing the true life stories of former American slaves — **as told by the ex-slaves themselves**. Interviewers working for the Work Projects Administration transcribed thousands of pages of these dialogues which now are housed in about six archival repositories throughout the United States. The former slaves ranged in age from their early seventies to well over one hundred years.

These interviews occurred during the late 1930's, a time of great economic depression in the United States. This depression affected everyone, especially America's poorest citizens, among whom were some of these formerly enslaved people. For many of those who had been treated humanely, remembrances of youthful days resurfaced with desires to return to times when food was plentiful. Those who had been abused knew that even the worst depression was a far better way of life.

SILVIA KING: Oh, I jes' can' 'member all dem good things us had in dem days. Sho' wish us had 'em now.

JENNY PROCTOR: Ise hear tell of dem good slave days but I ain't nev'r seen no good times den.

DONAVILLE BROUSSARD: I don't know whether it's been better since the war. I don't mean slavery was better than to be free. I mean times were better.

You will notice that the structure and spellings vary widely. While a few former slaves had gone on to attain college degrees, most remained almost, if not completely, illiterate. The skills of the writers conducting the interviews also ranged from excellent to barely adequate. Most of the slaves spoke like the uneducated Southern whites from whom they learned their speech patterns. Indeed, many whites, including some of the slaveowners themselves, were barely literate. A small number of slaves, especially the house slaves of well-educated whites, spoke grammatically correct English. Thus, it is difficult to determine if and when minor or extensive editing was done by the interviewers. Additionally, many were edited numerous times, creating several versions of the same dialogue. Other interviewers faithfully wrote their spellings of Southern dialect for every single word as pronounced by the ex-slaves.

Remember that discrimination and persecution were flourishing openly during the time of these interviews. The various attitudes directed towards these freed blacks by the interviewers — who were male and female, black and white — also affected the responses. (Most were white women.) Nevertheless, the majority of the ex-slaves were as candid as they dared to be and told significant amounts of details about their days in slavery.

CATO CARTER: Everythin' I tell you am the truth, but they's plenty I can't tell you.

As instructed to do, most writers followed the supplied questionnaire and queried their interviewees about a long list of topics, including ones such as their masters', parents', and siblings' names; treatment; work; food; and ghost stories. Others ignored the questionnaire procedure and let the ex-slaves have a free-flow conversation about any number of subjects.

As I compiled these precious words, I dared not do any extensive editing. I present them to you essentially as the interviewers wrote them, whether that was in dialect writing or in edited writing. Keep in mind that these writers often created several versions. I made very minor changes, such as correcting obvious typographical errors and adding or deleting *some* of the commas. I have included bits of information to you that I have enclosed [in brackets]. The interviewers' comments are enclosed (in parenthesis).

I am so pleased to present the following true life stories. Through them, we are able to learn much oral American history while enjoying the delicious Southern flavor of the words with which many of the slaves expressed themselves.

Blessings to you,

Jonna

Terminology

plantation = a large farming estate cultivated by workers producing crops and products for market

master or mistress = male or female slaveowner

quarters = slaves' cabins where they slept and sometimes ate

overseer = the person, almost always a white man, who had the duty of ensuring that the slaves completed all of their tasks, and of punishing the slaves (if allowed to do so by the owner); the overseer was hired by the owner, was a relative of the owner, was a slave of the owner, or was the slaveowner him or herself

pattyrollers, patterollers, patters = patrollers = white men, usually on horseback, who were hired by neighboring groups of slaveowners to patrol the areas surrounding the slaveowners' plantations at any time, but especially at night; the patrollers were paid to catch and whip slaves who were off their respective plantations without a written permission slip which was called a "pass"

pass = a permission slip, written by a slave's owner or overseer, which was required to be carried at all times by a slave when traveling anywhere not on the slaveowner's property; being caught without a pass could result in severe whippings or other punishments

potliquor, pot likker = liquid from food cooked in water, such as collard greens' liquid, making a flavorful and nutritious broth

half, halves, on the half or ha'f, shares = sharecropping = the sharing of the profits of farming; after Emancipation, some ex-slaveowners offered to supply the land and, if agreed, the ex-slaves supplied the labor to raise crops; the two shared the profits, usually 50% each, but sometimes the ex-slaves received only a third, or were deceived and received nothing

suit = a set or outfit of clothes; not a "suit" as the word is used currently; for slaves, this usually consisted of homespun clothing: a dress for women, pants and a shirt for men, and a dress (also called a shirt or shirttail) for both male and female children

slip = a straight dress; not underwear as the word is used currently

nigger = a term used during the time of slavery which referred to a slave or to a free black person and was used by both blacks and whites with little or no animosity (there were exceptions); currently used as an extremely derogatory and inflammatory term (there are exceptions)

nigger driver = a male slave who was the assistant to the overseer or performed the job instead of the overseer; also known as the overlooker

nigger trader = **slave trader** = almost exclusively, a white man whose business was buying, selling, trading, and often breeding slaves

refugeeing = fleeing to the West, usually to Texas, where slaves were taken by their owners who believed that there, in that state, they still could keep their slaves even if the Confederacy lost the Civil War

Juneteenth = June 19th = the name coined by former slaves meaning June 19, 1865, the date of the first time that many slaves were told of their freedom (which officially was proclaimed in the Emancipation Proclamation issued by President Abraham Lincoln in September 1862, which became effective on January 1, 1863); celebrated by ex-slaves yearly, beginning in 1866, as "Emancipation Day" in a few places, primarily in Texas; now observed nationally as an annual holiday with festivities by African Americans and many others

Ku Klux Klan = Klux, Klu Klux, Kluxers, Klan, KKK = an organization initially composed of Southern white males; members frequently wore white robes and hoods over their entire heads to conceal their identities; usually traveled by horseback at night; terrorized blacks, whites who were sympathetic to blacks, and others; terrorized by means of verbal and psychological abuse, beatings, whippings, destruction of property, human burnings, lynchings (hangings), and other forms of murder

hire out = the renting of slaves by their owners to other people to work for a day, month, year, or any period of time; the slave sometimes lived with the other person during the rental period

servant = a term often used to denote a slave who worked in or around the slaveowner's house, such as the cook, maid, butler, coachman, and other house slaves who were frequently (but not always) clothed, fed, and housed a little better than the field slaves

dinner = lunch **supper** = dinner

Dialect Glossary

ALSO SEE PAGES 7 AND 8

I have not tried to create a complete dialect glossary. It contains only the words most frequently used in this book series. Apostrophes vary widely. — Donna

ain't = am not, is not, are not, do (does, did) not, have (has) not, etc.

allers, allus = always

allus = all of us

atter = after

aw = all

ax = ask, asked

better'n = better than

brudder = brother

'cause, 'cose, 'caze, case = because

chillun, chillen = children

chap = child

clo's, close = clothes

'cose, corse, course = of course

cotch = catch, caught

cullud = colored

cum = come

dar = there

darsn't = dare not

dat = that

dawg = dog

day = they, their (sometimes day means day)

de = the

dem = them, those

den = then, than

dere, deir = their, there

dese = these

dey = they, their, there

dis = this

'do, do' = although; though; door

dose = those

effen = if

'em = them, him

en, en' = and

eny = any

er = a, an

er = or

et = ate

fer = for, far

fit = fought (sometimes fit means fit)

fo'ks = folks

froo = through

fur's = as far as

fust = first

Gawd = God

gib = give, gave

git = get

goobers = peanuts

gwine = going

hab = have

hafter = have to

hawg = hog

hit = it (sometimes hit means hit)

hoss = horse

iffen = if

Ise = I

Ise, I'se, I's, Ize = (I is) I am, I was, (I has) I have, etc.

jes', jis', jus' = just

jine, jin' = join

kaize, kaise = because

ketch = catch, caught

kin = can (sometimes kin means kin)

Kluxers = Ku Klux Klan (page 8)

lak = like

'lasses = molasses

Lawd = Lord

li'l = little

'lowed = said, declared; allowed

mai'ies = marry, marries

mammy = mother; also the title of the head house slave

Marster, marse, massa = master

mek = make, makes, made

Missus, missy, ol' miss, mistus = mistress

mo' = more

nigh = near

'nuff = enough

nuss = nursemaid; caregiver for children and the elderly (a <u>wet</u> nurse breastfed both black and white babies)
ob = of
onliest = only
pappy = father
patterrollers, pattyrollers, patters, patrolas = patrollers (page 7)
pickanninny, picanninney = a slave baby or toddler
plum = all; completely
po', pore = poor
quatahs = quarters = slaves' cabins
rations = food
sar = sir
sarbant, serbent = servant = house slave
sech, sich = such
set = sit, sat
sho, sho' = sure
slap = completely; all the way (sometimes slap means slap)
soon's = as soon as
sont = sent
sot = sat, set (sometimes sent)
suh = sir
sumpin' = something
'tain't = it is not, there are not, etc.
'taters = potatoes
ter = to
thar = there; their
they = their, there (sometimes they means they)
'tell, 'til = until

tote = carry
'twarn't = it was not, there were not, etc.
'twix, 'twixt = between
'twon't = it will not, there will not, etc.
tudder, tother, todder = the other
tuk = took
ub, uv = of
ud = would
udder, odder = other
uh = a, an
'um = him, them
us'n, us's = us, we, our
uster = used to
vittles, vittels = victuals = food
wah = war
warn't = was not, were not
w'en, wen = when
weuns, we'uns = we, us, our
whar = where
wid = with
w'ite, wite = white
wo'k, wuck, wuk, wukk = work
wuz = was, were
y'all, yawl = you all (the plural of you)
yas = yes
yes'm, yes'um = yes madam
yo' = you, your
younguns = children
yous, youse = you, your
yuh = you, your
'zactly = exactly

An apostrophe (') indicates that one or more letters are missing from a word:

buildin's = buildings
he'p = help

can' = can't
'lect = recollect

f'om = from
fo' = for

-ah = -er or -r when used at the end of a word:

fouah = four
heah = hear

ordah = order
flooah = floor

powah = power
buttah = butter

DESCRIPTIONS OF PLANTATION LIFE
— Excerpts from Full Life Stories —

You frequently will notice that one person gives some information immediately followed by __another person who says the exact opposite.__ Both can be correct since there was no standard or "average" plantation. Each plantation was as different as its owner.

*The following photographs are of **real** slave cabins and other items from the time of slavery. Photographs have been chosen to show examples of items described by interviewees but are not necessarily the same items used by the interviewees.*

PLEASE UNDERSTAND:
I'm continuously locating photographs, many of which never have been published. There is not an abundance of photographs of slaves and only a few of the ex-slaves had their photos taken during the interviews in the 1930's. As a result, some of the same photographs are repeated in different books. — Donna

JACOB BRANCH: Slavery, one to 'nother, was purty rough. Every plantation have to answer for itself.

11

HOUSING

Window hole with swinging door

LEWIS JONES: Weuns live in de cullud quatahs. Dem am long cabins wid a dirt flooah [floor] an' a hole in de wall fo' a windah [window] widout glass. Weuns sleep on bunks wid straw ticks [mattresses].

MARGARETT NILLIAN: Dere was no windah in de cabin, jus' a hole wid a swingin' dooah. Ob co'se, dat lets de flies in durin' de summah, an' de col' in durin' de wintah. Dey could shut de dooah of de windah, but dat shut out de light.

SUSAN FORREST: De way de place was 'ranged (arranged), dey [there] was de Big House w'ere de marster live, den behin' was a row of 'bout fifteen or twenty cabin on one side and another row of fifteen or twenty cabin on de other side.

JEFF CALHOUN: We makes our beds out of forked saplings drove in the ground 'cause de floors was dirt. We sets de pole in dat ground and it run to de top of de cabin. We makes one bed down low and one bed above. De big folks sleeps in de low beds and de chillun above 'cause dey can climb.

LOUIS FOWLER: De cabins am two an' some three rooms. Dey am built ob logs an' chinked wid a piece of wood an' daubed wid dirt to fill de cracks. De way weuns fix de dirt am dis-a-way [this way]: Weuns took sich dirt as de clay or de gumbo which am sticky when it am wet. Dat dirt am soaked wid wautah 'til it sticks togedder. Weuns also mix hay or straw wid it. W'en sich mud am daubed in de cracks 'twix de logs, it stays. Dem cabins sho' am windproof an' wahm [warm].

LOUIS CAIN: Our quarters was made of logs in a long shed [that was] six rooms long, like cow sheds or chicken houses.

WILL LONG: De wind in de winter comes through de crevices an' between de logs. De chimbleys wuz made ob sticks an' sometimes de wind come through an' set de stick chimbly on fire.

Log and plank cabins with mud chimneys

RICHARD CARRUTHERS: The niggers had log cabins and they burned down often times. The chimney would cotch fire 'cause it was made out of sticks and clay and moss. Many the time we have to git up at midnight and push the chimney 'way from the house to keep the house from burnin' up.

CLARA BRIM: Some of de houses was log houses and some was buil' outer plank, but dey was all good houses. Dey wasn' jis' put togedder any way, but dey was well-built. Dey had brick chimneys.

AUSTIN GRANT: The beds was one of your own make. If you knowed how to make one, you had one. Of course, the chillen slept on the floor, patched up some way.

VALMAR CORMIER: De slave house was jes' a old plank house 'bout twelve feet by twenty feet and have dirt floor.

JACK MADDOX: [The baby was kept warm in the cook's bed]. But my other brothers and sisters had to sleep on the floor in the cabin huddled together in cold weather so we wouldn't freeze to death. Our life was misery.

ANNIE ROW: In summertime, mos' de cullud folks sleeps outside. Weuns had to fight mosquitoes in de night and flies in de day. They [There] was flies and then some more flies, and with all deir relations, in them cabins.

JAMES CALHART JAMES: I was a half-brother to the [white] children of the Randolphs, four in number. After I was born, mother and I lived in the servants' quarters of the Big House, enjoying many pleasures that the other slaves did not: eating and sleeping in the Big House, playing and associating with my half-brothers and sisters. We lived in a large white frame house containing about 15 rooms with every luxury of that day, my father being very rich. I have heard the Randolph's plantation contained about 4,000 acres and about 300 slaves.

Servants' quarters, in this example not attached to the Big House

THOMAS COLE: We [he, brother, and sister] lived in one room of the Big House and allus had a good bed to sleep in and good things to eat at the same table, after de white folks gits through.

LU PERKINS: I stayed in the [slaveowner's] house. I slep' in the little trundle bed that they pulled out from under the bed at night. The coldest nights, the old missus took me in the bed with her. I uster curl up down at the foot and sleep warm and comfable as a kitten in a basket.

FOOD

FLORENCE NAPIER: Ise sho' 'joy myse'f on de old plantation, an' weuns all had a good time. Allus have plenty to eat. Marster use to says, "De cullud fo'ks raised de food an' dey's 'titled to all dey wants." Same wid de clothes. W'en de marster says de cullud fo'ks raised de food, 'twas true fo' sho'. Ever'thin' on de place weuns raised right dere. All de meat, veg'tables, co'n, fruit, an' sich, an' all de cloth an' de clothes am made right thar. No, sar, 'twarn't much de marster have to buy.

WILLIAM MOORE: We had a purty hard time to make out and was hongry lots of times. Marse Tom didn't feel called on to feed his hands any too much. I 'members I had a cravin' for victuals [food] all the time. I'd take lunches to the field hands and they'd say, "Lawd, Gawd, it ain't 'nough to stop the grip in you belly." We made out on things from the fields and rabbits cooked in li'l fires.

HAGAR LEWIS: Some pore niggahs were half-starved. They belonged to other people [from nearby plantations or farms]. Miss Mary would call the niggahs in to feed 'em, see 'em outside the fence picking up scraps. They'd call out at night, "Marse John! Marse John!" They's afraid to come in daytime. Marse John'd say, "What's the matter now, Andrew" or Jim or someone's name. "Ise hongry." He'd say, "Come on in and git it." He knew they was half-feedin' 'em.

LU PERKINS: They [There] was 'bout a hunderd colored folks on Judge Hooker's place but you didn't hear of no hungerin' or sufferin'. I can 'member the times when they kill a hundred head of hogs at one time on that place. He had a hunderd cows and churned three times a day.

LEWIS JONES: Marster Tate don't give the rations to each fam'ly lak lots ob udder marsters do. Him have de cookhouse an' de cooks. All de rations am cooked by dem an' allus [all of us] sat down to de long tables fo' to eat de meals. Dere am plenty, plenty. Yas, sar, plenty good rations. I's sho' wish I's could have good rations lak dat now. Man, some of dat ham would go fine. Dat was "ham w'at am!"

KATIE DARLING: We et [ate] peas and greens and collards and middlin's [cheap parts of pork]. Niggers had better let that ham alone!

ELLEN BUTLER: Old Massa didn't give 'em much to eat. When they comes in out of the field, they goes [to] work for other folks for something to eat.

No cooking in cabins:

HAGAR LEWIS: They [Their] big cooking was done all together. Mamma cooked it all in the same place for white folks and us.

JOHN FINNELY: Dere was no cookin' done in de cabins on de marster's place. De cookin' am done in de cookhouse by de cooks fo' allus niggers. Weuns et in de eatin' shed.

VICTOR DUHON: Master had about 100 acres in cotton and the corn. He had a slave for to hunt all the time. He didn't do other things. The partridge and the rice birds he killed were cooked for the white folks. The owls and the rabbits and the 'coons [raccoons] and the 'possums were cooked for us. They had a big room for us to eat in. Where they cook, they had a long oven with a piece down the middle. They cooked the white folks' things on one side. They cooked their own things on the other. They had each one's pots and skillets.

Cooking in cabins:

AARON RUSSEL: Every cabin does dey own cookin'. Breakfust must be over in time to be in de field, or de shop, or whar de wo'k am befo' daylight. Ise know some of de plantations have all de slaves eat in one place, but de marster lets every couple have de home an' he measures out de ration once a week.

ISOM NORRIS: Ever' Sunday mo'ning, we all went to the Big House to get our week's supply of food. We got plenty to last us until the next Sunday, such as meat, flour, lard, peas, beans, potatoes and syrup.

GUS JOHNSON: Dey give de rations on Saturday and dat's 'bout five pound salt bacon and a peck of meal and some sorghum syrup. Dey make dat syrup on the plantation. We have lots to eat, and if the rations run short, we goes huntin' or fishin'. Some de old men kills rattlesnake and cook 'em like fish and say dey fish. I eat dat many a time and never knowed it. 'Twas good, too.

ANNIE ROW: De food am mostly cornmeal and 'lasses [molasses] and meat that am weighed out and has to last you de week. De truth am, lots of time weuns goes hungry. Everything dat am worn and eat was raised on de place, 'cept salt and pepper and stuff like that. Dey raise de cotton and de wheat, and de corn and de cane, 'sides de fruit and sich, and de chickens and de sheep and de cows and de hawgs.

ANNA MILLER: We keeps full on what we gits, such as beans, co'nmeal and 'lasses. We seldom gits meat. White flour — we don't know what dat taste like.

TOB DAVIS: Thar am no limit to de fresh meat weuns would have. 'Twas good meat. It had a good flavor an' am tender. Tudder food am veg'tables, all de 'taters weuns wants, an', in the summahtime, all de fresh veg'tables. De bread am co'n, mostly. Thar am some white flouah, 'nough fo' one batch of biscuits a week. Sho', de good old 'lasses an' honey, an' plenty of it, also brown sugar. De marster have lots of beehives. Thar am milk an' buttah, all weuns wants of it, too.

ANNA MILLER: We gits 'bout all de milk we wants 'cause dey puts it in de trough and we helps ourselves. Dere was a trough for de niggers and one for de hawgs.

MARY REYNOLDS: They brought the vittles [food] and the water to the fields on a slide pulled by a old mule. Plenty times they was only a half barrel of water and it stale and hot for all the niggers on the hottest days. Mostly we ate pickled pork, cornbread, peas, beans and 'taters. They never was as much as we needed.

JACK WHITE: Mos' of de time, in dem day, us lib on co'nbread, peas, an' sweet 'taters. Marster was a Mef'dis' preacher. W'en he'd go off to preach, Mistress hire us [out to other white people] to pick cotton [and gave us] a biscuit apiece. We prize dat biscuit so. We'd hang it up on a stalk of cotton an' watch it, an' eb'ry now an' den, go back an' tek a bite offn it. Us all git a biscuit Sunday mo'ning, too. Us neber go huntin' for 'possom an' rabbit like de other niggers did.

JEFF CALHOUN: We allus had lots to eat, but for meat, we has to go to de woods [in Texas] and git deer and turkey and buffalo and some bear. I have eat hoss [horse] and skunk and crow and hawk. We has a big fire to cook on. To make de corncakes, we put one leaf down and put batter on dat and put another leaf over it and cover with hot ashes and by noon it was done. Same thing for supper. We never have biscuits 'cept on Sunday or Christmas.

JIM FRANKLIN: In slav'ry day, we didn' hab nuttin' to eat t'roo [through] the week but cawnbread and sweet 'taters. On Sunday, we git one biscuit apiece, and I tells you, it taste' better'n cake do now.

TOB DAVIS: Mostest de cookin' in de summahtime am done in de yard 'less it rains. De cookin' am done in de fireplace in de wintahtime.

VALMAR CORMIER: Us cook in de big fireplace and take a log 'bout four feet long and have a big iron pot with a iron lid. Dey put red hot coals under de pot and on top de lid. Dey have a big iron poker with a hook on it what dey took de lid off with.

SILVIA KING: An' de smokehouse hit [it] full of bacon sides an' cured hams an' barrels of 'lasses an' lard. Everytime er nigger want ter eat, all he do jes' ask an' git his passel (portion) out.

WES BRADY: If we et flour bread, our woman folks had to slip the flour siftin's from Missy's kitchen and darsn't [dare not] let the white folks know it.

SILVIA KING: Some dat us had to eat den ud [would] sho' be good eatin' fer er millunyare now. Wild turkey, bar [bear], deer an' sech. In de diff'unt fruit seasons, all de wimmin mos' on de place er wukin' from 'fore daylight 'til late at night, dryin' an' 'zarvin' [preserving food] an' de lak.

19

JOHN SNEED: Us had 'possum and rabbit and fish and trap birds for eatin'. Dere all kind wild greens dem days. Us jus' go in de woods and git wild lettuce and mustard and leatherbritches and polk salad and watercress, all us want to eat. Each family have de li'l garden and raise turnips and cabbage and sweet 'taters and put dem in de kiln make from cornstalks and cure dem for winter eatin'.

GREEN CUMBY: We mos'ly lives on cornpone and slab bacon de marster give us. We didn't have no gardens ourselves 'cause we wouldn't have time to work in dem. We worked all day in the fields and den was so tired we couldn't do nothin' more.

LORENA EZELL: All de man folks was 'lowed [to] raise a garden patch with tobaccy or cotton for to sell in de market. Wasn't many massas what 'lowed deir niggers have patches and some didn't even feed 'em enough. Dat's why dey have to git out and hustle [steal] at night to git food for dem to eat.

RICHARD CARRUTHERS: If they didn't provision you 'nough, you jus' had to slip 'round and git a chicken. That ain't stealin', is it? You has to keep right on workin' in the field if you ain't 'lowanced 'nough. No nigger like to work with his belly groanin'.

STEVE CONNALLY: Dey didn't have no 'frigerators den, but dey built log houses without a floor over de good, cold spring, and put flat rocks dere to keep de milk and cream and butter cold.

Ice house in Virginia used to keep foods cold

TOM MILLS: My mother done the cookin' up at the [slaveowner's] house because she was workin' up there all the time, weavin' cloth and, of course, we ate up there. The rest of 'em didn't like it much because we ate up there, but her work was there. I don't know what the other slaves had to eat. They cooked for themselves. But we had jes' what the Pattersons had to eat. On Sunday mornin', we had flour bread. We made the co'nmeal right on the place. We made chittlin's (chitterlings). We dried beef, strung it out, and put it on the line. We had lots of deer and turkeys, quail and 'possums, but they never did do much eatin' rabbits.

SARAH FORD: I guess Massa Charles, what taken us when Massa Kit die, was 'bout the same as all white folks what owned slaves, some good and some bad. We had plenty to eat — more'n I has now — and plenty clothes and shoes. And even does your stomach be full, and does you have plenty clothes, dat bullwhip on your bare hide make you forgit de good part, and dat's de truth.

CLOTHING

WILLIAM BRANCH: How'd us slaves git de clothes? We carded de cotton, den de women spin it on a spinnin' wheel. After dat, day sew de gahment togeddah on a sewin' machine. Yahsur [Yes, sir], we's got sewin' machine, wid a big wheel and a handle. One woman tu'n de handle and de yuther woman do de sewin'. Dat's how we git de clothes for de 75 slaves. Marster's clothes? We makes dem for de whole fam'ly. De missis send de pattern and de slaves makes de clothes. Over nigh [near] Richmond, a frien' of Marster Woodson has 300 slaves. Dey makes all de clothes for dem.

ANNIE OSBORNE: I had one dress the year 'round, two lengths of cloth sewed together. Massa fed well 'nough, but made us wear our old lowel clothes 'til they 'most fell off us. We was treated jus' like animals, but some owners treated they stock better'n old Tom Bias handled my folks.

ANDREW GOODMAN: They made us plenty of good clothes. In summer, we wore long shirts, split up the sides, made out of lowerings

— that's same as cotton sacks was made out of. In winter, we had good jeans and knitted sweaters and knitted socks.

ANNA MILLER: Weuns makes all de cloth for to makes de clothes, but we don't git 'em. In de winter, we 'mos' freeze to death.

GILL RUFFIN: They give us one garment at a time and that had to be slap [completely] wore-out 'fore we got another. All us niggers went barefoot. I never seen a nigger with shoes on 'til after de surrender.

WILL RHYMES: Marster didn' furnish the chaps [children] no shoes.

MARY REYNOLDS: In them days, I wore shirts like all the young girls and boys. They was made with collars like boys have today and they come below the knees and were split up the sides. That's all we wore in hot weather. The older men wore jeans and the womens wore ginghams. Shoes was the worstest trouble. We wore rough russets when it got cold and it seems powerful strange that they never could get them to fit. Once when I was a young gal, they got me a new pair and they was all brass studded in the toes and in the heels and ankles. They was too little for me but I had to wear them. The brass cut into my ankles and the places got miserable bad. I rubbed tallow in the sore places and wropped rags around my ankles and worked in the fields and my sores got worser and worser. The scars are there to this day. I thought my feet would rot off of me.

WILLIS EASTER: All us chillen weared lowel white duckin', homemake, jes' one garment. It was de long shirt. You couldn't tell gals from boys on the yard.

JOHN SNEED: Us have homemake clothes and brogan shoes, come from Austin or some place. Us chillen wear shirttail 'til us 'bout thirteen.

ZEK BROWN: Ise 'membahs de last dress Ise wore. 'Twas a linsey cloth, lak homespun am, wid stripes. Dat am de last dress. Aftah dat, Ise put in pants.

BUD JONES: I weared split shirts 'til I was nearly growed. I wanted me a little pair of pants, but I'm tellin' the truth when I say I didn't wear nothin' [as a small child] — nothin' a-tall [at all] for the most part, 'cept that shirt. I went in the snow barefoot. When I was bigger, they got me brass stud shoes and a hat once a year, but no pants.

LOUIS LOVE: De clothes us wore was shirts and us didn't git no britches 'til us big. I's wearin' britches a good many year 'fore freedom, though. Dey give us two suit [sets of clothes] de year and us have beefhide shoes what us call moc'sins [in Texas].

KATIE PHOENIX: My father made shoes. He would send mine over to me. They was good and not red russets like I learn later niggers was lucky to get.

JOHN CRAWFORD: The [white] chillens and grandchillens of Grandpappy [the slaveowner] went to school in a carriage all dressed fine. Mammy allus had to button they boots. It outdone [angered] her 'cause her chillens had to go barefoot and crack they heels open and have the ground itch in they feet. Grandpappy made a trip to New Orleans to git his special-made boots.

AUSTIN GRANT: We went barefooted in the summer and winter, too. You had to prepare that for yourself. If you didn't have head enough to prepare for yourself, you went without.

ISAAC MARTIN: Dey had a time to call all de slaves up and give 'em hats, and anudder time dey give 'em shoes, and anudder time dey give 'em clo's [clothes]. Dey see dat eb'rybody was fit.

KATIE DARLING: Us got two pieces of clothes for winter and two for summer, but us have no shoes.

JEFF CALHOUN: We never wore no shoes in de summer and some winters neither. We has a good pair of pants and shirt we wears Sundays and holidays and was married in.

THOMAS JOHNS: We wore some cotton clothes in de summer but in de winter we wore wool clothes. We allus had shoes. A shoemaker would come 'round once a year and stay maybe 30 days, makin' shoes for everybody on de place. Den in about 6 months, he would come back and half-sole and make other repairs to de shoes. We made all our clothes on de place. We wove light wool cloth for summer and heavy for winter.

JACK MADDOX: But shoes, underwear, a bed, a hat was things I didn't know nothing 'bout 'til I was along sixteen years old.

JULIA DANIELS: Unnerwear? I ain't never wore no unnerwear then.

TOB DAVIS: All the shoes am made f'om de hides of all de critters killed on de place.

PREELY COLEMAN: Massa Tom made us wear shoes 'cause they's so many snags and stumps our feet gits sore. They was red russet shoes. I'll never forgit 'em. They was so stiff at first we could hardly stand 'em.

RICHARD CARRUTHERS: Come a nother [wind] and it blow with snow and sleet and I didn't have 'nough clothes to keep me warm.

WILLIS WOODSON: I stays in de [slaveowner's] house, so I gets good clothes and shoes, too. Some dem niggers didn't have hardly no clothes, though.

ANNIE YOUNG HENSON: My position was second nurse [probably nursemaid, not medical nurse] for the doctor's family, or one of the inner servants of the family, not one of the field hands. In my position, my clothes were made better, and better quality than the others, all made and arranged to suit the mistress' taste. I got a few things of feminine dainty that was discarded by the mistress, but no money, nor did I have any to spend.

FIELD AND NIGHT WORK

JULIA MALONE: 'Twas 'bout 1,000 acres in de place. I's don't know 'bout de numbah of slaves on de place, but 'twas so many gwine an' comin' dat 'peared lak de beehive. 'Twas so many buildin's an' sheds on de place dat [it] looked lak a small town.

SUSAN MERRIT: The hands was woke with the big bell [see page 59] and when Massa pulls that bell rope, the niggers falls out them bunks like rain fallin'. They was in that field 'fore day and stay 'til dusk dark. They work slap [completely] up 'til Saturday night.

NELSON DAVIS: Ebery mornin' de slaves wuz woked up erbout four o'clock an' sont ter de fields ter plough, hoe, cut brush er firewood and sech. Dey allers wuked 'twil erbout dusk.

THOMAS COLE: We'd git up early every day in de year, rain or shine, hot or cold. A slave blowed de horn and dere no danger of you not wakin' up when dat blowed long and loud. He climb up on a platform 'bout ten feet tall to blow dat bugle. We'd work 'til noon and eat in de shade and rest 'bout a hour or a little more iffen it hot, but only a hour if it cold. You is allus tired when you makes de day like dat on de plantation.

STEVE ROBERTSON: De cotton dat am growed on de place am a sight fo' sho'. Ise can almost see de white fields now. Deys picks de cotton an' puts it in big wickah baskets. Ise can see dem old fo'ks comin' in f'om de field now, wid de big basket dat am tallah dan some ob de chilluns, on top de head.

MARY REYNOLDS: The times I hated most was pickin' cotton when the frost was on the bolls. My hands would get so sore that they would crack open and bleed. We would have a little fire in the fields and iffen the ones with tender hands couldn't stan' it no longer, we would run and warm our hands a little bit.

THOMAS JOHNS: Well, when de cotton firs' open and hadn't dried out, a man could pick two hun'erd poun's ever' day. But when de cotton had had time to dry out and, course, didn't weigh so much, he maybe couldn't pick his two hun'erd poun's or whatever de 'mount wuz set for him to pick. Den dey'd beat him 'cause he didn' pick what dey tol' him to. After de cotton wuz ginned, it had to be baled. Dey would make deir niggers wuk right on from de time it got too dark to see how to pick cotton, without no supper, balin' cotton even if it tuk 'til four o'clock in de mornin'.

SUSAN FORREST: Dey hab de slaves out 'til ten 'clock at night wukin' 'em, sometime.

ANNIE LITTLE: In the cold winter, we woman would spin on de ole spinnin' wheel, an' weave de cloth on de looms. I 'members how I would stand by de looms an' pick up de shuttles w'en dey fell to de flo' [floor]. We niggers all wore de clos' [clothes] dat they make on de spinnin' wheel, but de white folks wear dresses bot [bought] from de sto' [store] sometime.

GILL RUFFIN: On rainy days, we was in de crib shuckin' corn.

ANDREW GOODMAN: He didn't never put the niggers out in bad weather. He give us something to do, in out of the weather, like shellin' corn and the woman could spin and knit.

AARON RUSSEL: If 'twas lots of rain weather an' deys can't plow an' gets behind, den deys work Saturday aftahnoon an' Sunday if necessary to catch up.

ELLEN PAYNE: The hands worked from sun-up 'til sun-down. When they come in at night, 'most everyone had a task to do. Some spin, or make baskets or chair bottoms, or knit socks.

ANNA MILLER: De weavin' was de night work, after workin' all de day in de fiel'.

SILVIA KING: In de winter ebenin's [evenings], de men an' boys would sit 'roun' de fire an' whittle out things or make nets an' seines to fish wid an' de wimmin ud sew, er spin, er weave, but not much weavin' at night 'case it wuz by candlelight er a pine [knot] torch an' dey couldn't see much. De ole folks ud tell tales an' de young ones ud whittle, patch harness, or pick cotton offen de seed.

WILLIS EASTER: All de lint was picked by hand on our place. It a slow job to git dat lint out de cotton and I's gone to sleep many a night, settin' by de fire, pickin' lint. In bad weather, us sot by de fire and pick lint and patch harness and shoes, or whittle out something, dishes and bowls and troughs and traps and spoons.

TIME OFF

JACOB BRANCH: Sunday de onliest rest day.

KATIE DARLING: We have to work Saturday all day and if that grass was in the field, we didn't git no Sunday, either.

ADELINE CUNNINGHAM: No, suh, we ain't got no holidays. Sundays we grinds co'n and de men split rails and hoes wid de grubbin' hoe.

LOUIS CAIN: On Saturday night, we'd have a dance all night long. Sunday, the men went to see they wives or sweethearts [on neighboring plantations] and us younguns went swimmin' in the creek.

GILL RUFFIN: We worked every day 'cept Sunday and didn't know any more 'bout a holiday dan climbin' up a tree back'ard. He never let us have parties. Sometimes we went fishin' or huntin' on Sat'day afternoon, but that wasn't often.

MARY REYNOLDS: Once in awhile, they would give us a little piece of Saturday evenin's to wash our clothes in the branch. We hung them on the groun' in the woods to dry. There was a place to wash clothes from the well, but they was so many niggers that all couldn't get 'round to it on Sundays.

AUSTIN GRANT: On Saturday nights, we jes' knocked 'round the place.

STEVE ROBERTSON: Now, 'bout de 'musements on de place. 'Twarn't no pahties nor gwine to chu'ch fo' de niggers.

ANDREW GOODMAN: He [the slaveowner] built us a church. A old man, Kenneth Lyons, who was a slave of the Lyons family nearby, used to git a pass every Sunday mornin' and come preach to us.

Much more information about churches is in Book 19: Religion, Songs, and Communications.

HATTIE COLE: No, sar, no, sar! Thar am no parties on Marster's plantation. Him says 'tain't fo' parties he have de plantation, but 'tis fo' wo'k.

CLARA BRIM: Dey neber was no dancin' on de place. I neber l'arn how to dance.

ANNIE ROW: Dey neber give de cullud folks de pass for to go a-visiting, nor 'lows parties on de place.

KATIE DARLING: They have dances and parties for the white folks' chillen, but Missy say, "Niggers was made to work for white folks."

JOHN FINNELY: Yous wants me to tell 'bout de 'joyments on de plantation? Dere was no pahties or dancin' but weuns have de co'n [corn] huskin' an' de nigger fights. De co'n huskin' am w'en de cullud fo'ks ob de neighbahood come to one place an' j'in in de huskin' ob de co'n. De nigger fights am mo' fo' de w'ite fo'ks' 'joyment but allus niggers am 'lowed to see it. De marsters ob de diffe'nt planta-tions match deir niggers 'cordin' to size, an' den bet on dem.

MARTIN RUFFIN: Cornshuckings was a big occasion them days and Massa give all the hands a quart whiskey apiece. They'd drink whiskey, get happy and make more noise than a little, but better not git drunk. We'd dance all night when cornshuckin' was over.

ANDREW GOODMAN: Once a week, the slaves could have any night they want for a dance or frolic. Mance McQueen was a slave 'longing on the Dewberry place, what could play a fiddle, and his master give him a pass to come play for us. Marse Bob give us chickens or kilt a fresh beef or let us make 'lasses candy. We could choose any night, 'cept in the fall of the year. Then we worked awful hard and didn't have the time. We had a gin run by horsepower. After sundown when we left the fields, we used to gin a bale of cotton every night. We allus got Saturday afternoons off to fish and hunt. We used to have fish frys and plenty game in them days.

GREEN CUMBY: Other times at night, de slaves gathers 'round de cabins in little bunches and talks 'til bedtime. Sometimes we'd dance and someone would knock out time for us by snappin' de fingers and slappin' de knee. We didn't have nothin' to make de music on.

JOHN SNEED: After work, de old folks sot 'round, fiddle and play de 'cordian and tell stories. Dat mostly after de crops laid by or on rainy days. On workin' time, dey usually tired and go to bed early. Dey not work on Saturday afternoon or Sunday, 'cept dey gatherin' de crop 'gin' a [against an impending] rain. Old man Jim Piper am fiddler and play for black and white dances.

FRED BROWN: Weuns am 'lowed to have de parties an' de dances. Weuns have fo' de music, sich as de banjo, jew's harp, an' de 'cordian, an' fo' de time, dey beat de piece ob steel. Dey dance de ol' fashion dance, de promenade, an' de jog. Sometimes dey have de jiggin' contest. Two niggers puts a glass ob wauter on deir heads an' den see who can dance de hardest widout spillin' any wauter. Den 'twas de log rollin'. Dat am de contest 'tween two teams, 'bout three to de team. Dey see which can roll de log de fastest.

LU PERKINS: Then they got to singin' war songs. Every night, the judge and the old missus had the niggers come to the Big House and stand in rows in they clean lowerings clothes with white handkerchiefs tied 'round they heads and have play-party songs.

JACK WHITE: In slav'ry days, hol'days didn' 'mount to much. Dey gib us flour to bake a cake on Crissmus day.

LOUIS FOWLER: De big doin's am on Christmas Day. On that day, de marster have a present fo' each cullud person. De presents am simple things. Ise laugh now w'en Ise think ob dem. But de cullud fo'ks sho' 'joy deir presents, an' it showed de marster's heart am right. Fo' de chilluns, it am candy. Fo' de womens, it am a pin or sich, an' fo' de men, it am a knife or sich.

ANDERSON EDWARDS: Gen'rally Christmas was like any other day. But I got Santa Claus twict in slavery 'cause Massa give me a sack [bag] of molasses candy once and some biscuits once. That a whole lot to me then.

AUSTIN GRANT: Christmas? I don't know as I was ever home Christmas. My boss kep' me hired out [rented out to other people]. The slaves never had no Christmas presents I know of. And big dinners, I never was at nary one. They didn't give us nothin', I tell you, but a grubbin' hoe and axe and the whip.

MARY REYNOLDS: Christmas was the best time of the year. No matter what day in the week it come on, we don't have to work. They give all the niggers fresh meat on that day and, them that uses it, a plug of tobacco around.

JEFF CALHOUN: De only time we got to rest was Sunday and de Fourth of July and Christmas, and one day Thanksgiving. We got de big dinners on [those] holidays.

LOUIS CAIN: On Christmas [as a child], I'd stand by the gate to open it for the company, and they'd throw nuts and candy to me. That night, all the slaves what could, brung they banjoes and fiddles and played for the white folks to dance all night.

SYLVESTER BROOKS: We serenade dem [white folks] an' dey has us ter cum on in an' help ourselves to de cake or wine or whatever dey has fer us ter eat or drink. We do dis ebery Chrismus and Thanksgivin'.

DIFFERENCES IN PLANTATIONS

To some slaves, life on the plantation was tolerable; to others, it was cruel and pain-laden. The courses of their lives were extremely varied, being completely dependent upon decisions made by their owners.

CATO CARTER: Back in Alabama, Missie Adeline Carter took me when I was past my creepin' [crawling] days to live in the Big House with the white folks. I had a room built on the Big House [slaveowner's house] where I stayed. They was allus good to me 'cause I's one of their blood.

Talkin' 'bout victuals, our eatin' was good. Can't say the same for all places. Some of the plantations half-starved their niggers and 'lowanced out their eatin' 'til they wasn't fittin' for work. They had to slip about to niggers on other places to piece out their meals.

My massa used to give me a li'l money 'long to buy what I wanted. I allus bought fine clothes. In the summer when I was a li'l one, I wore lowerin's like the rest of the niggers. That was things made from cotton sackin'. Most the boys wore shirttails 'til they was big yearlin's. When they bought me red russets from the town, I cried and cried. I didn't want to wear no rawhide shoes. So they took 'em back. They had a weakness for my cryin'. I did have plenty fine clothes, good woolen suits they spinned on the place, and doeskins and fine linens. I druv in the car'age [carriage] with the white folks and was 'bout the mos' dudish nigger in them parts.

TEMPIE CUMMINS: Miss Fannie Neyland, she Mis' Phil Scarborough now, she raise me 'cause I was give to them when I was eight year old.

I slep' on a pallet on the floor. They give me a homespun dress onct a year at Christmas time. When company come, I had to run and slip on that dress. At other time, I wore white chillens' cast-off clothes, so wore [worn] they was ready to throw away. I had to pin them up with red horse thorns to hide my nakedness. My dress was usually split from hem to neck and I had to wear them 'til they was strings. Went barefoot summer and winter 'til the feets crack open.

At mealtime, they hand me a piece of cornbread and tell me "Run 'long." Sometime I git little piece of meat and biscuit, 'bout onct a month. I gathered up scraps the white chillens lef'.

The white chillen tries [to] teach me to read and write, but I didn' larn much 'cause I allus workin'.

31

BETTY POWERS

Betty Powers at time of interview

What fo' yous wants dis old nigger's story 'bout old slave'y days? 'Tain't worth anything. Ise jus' hard wo'kin' person all my life. Raised de fam'ly, an' does right as best as Ise can by dem.

Now, to tell de truth 'bout my age, Ise don't know 'zactly. Ise 'membahs de war [the Civil War] time, an' de surrendah time. Ise old 'nough to fan flies off de white fo'ks an' off de tables w'en dey eats w'en surrendah comes. Ise 'membahs 'cause 'tis de fust whuppin' Ise gits. 'Twas once w'en Ise failed to see some flies on de table an' de marster had comp'ny fo' dinnah. De daughter tooks me upstairs an' use de whup [whip] on me. Mary am her name.

Yas, sar, Ise do de bestest I can to 'membahs fo' yous. If yous come 'bout five yeahs ago, Ise could tell lots mo', but de last five yeahs,

Ise had de head misery. My brain goes to wautah [water], so dat 'fects de mind.

Ise bo'n in Harrison County, Texas. 'Twas 'bout 25 miles f'om Marshall. Ise 'membahs dat 'cause de marster says 'twas dat, an', co'se, Ise lives in dat country 'til Ise grows up. Weuns warn't far f'om Weziana.

Marster's name am Doctah [Doctor] Howard Perry. He am a doctah, so his wife an' de overseer looks after de place, an' sees 'bout de wo'k while he am 'way. Next to de marster's house am a small buildin' dat am used fo' de office. De missy am in thar mostest of de time. De cullud fo'ks warn't 'lowed to go to de house. If weuns wants to see de marster or his wife, weuns have to go to de office.

De plantation am awful big one. How many acres? Gosh fo' Mighty! Why, 'twas mo' dan Ise could count. If yous ask how many miles 'twas long, den m'ybe miles could be told, but Ise fo'gits de miles. De wautah on my brain spoils my 'collection. De numbah of slaves am somethin' 'gains Ise fo'gits. Ise never 'membahs heahin' [hearing]. M'ybe no one knows. 'Twas a whole lot, I knows 'twas mo' den 200.

De cullud fo'ks lives in de cabins. 'Twas called de quatahs [quarters]. Now, in each cabin lives one fam'ly. 'Twas de father, mother an' de chilluns. Thar am 'bout as many chilluns as thar am grown-ups. Ise can shut my eyes now an' see dem rows of cabins. Thar am three rows, an' de rows am 'bout ha'f a mile long. Ever' fam'ly does its own cookin'. Mammy, pappy, an' deir 12 chilluns lives in our cabin, so mammy have to cook fo' 14 people, 'sides her field work. She am up 'way befo' daylight in de mo'nin' an' fixin' de breakfast, an' de suppah am fixed after dark. Dey have to use de pine-knot torch fo' to make de light so dey can see. De cookin' am done in de fireplace in de wintahtime, an' in de yard mostest of de summahtime.

All de rations am measured out on Sunday mo'nin'. What am given have to do 'til next Sunday. Thar am plenty diffe'nt rations, but 'twarn't 'nough fo' de heavy eaters. Weuns all have to be real careful, an' den some of de fo'ks goes hongry sometimes. De marster gives weuns meat, co'n [corn] meal, 'lasses, p'taters, peas, beans, milk, an' weuns gits white flouah on Sunday mo'nin'. Jus' 'nough fo' to make one batch of biscuits.

De short [small quantities of] rations caused lots of trouble 'cause de niggers have to steal food. 'Twas a whuppin' if dey gits catched. De cullud fo'ks am in a hell of a fix if dey can't do de wo'k 'cause dey am weak, even if dey am hongry. 'Twas a whuppin' den fo' sho' [for sure]. If dey steals de food so dey stays strong an' can do de task, 'twas a whuppin'. So thar 'twas. [So, there it was.] Mostest of dem steals an' tooks a whuppin' if dey am catched, an' on a full stomach. My fo'ks don't have to steal food, but weuns am careful. Yous can jus' bet 'twarn't nothin' wasted.

None of de infants suffers fo' de want of food, 'cause dey am fed twice a day in de nursery. Dat am de place whar de younguns am left by de mothers while dey am at wo'k. De infants gits plenty of food. 'Twas mostly milk wid co'nbread crumbled up in it, an' potliquor [liquid from cooked greens] wid co'nbread fixed de same way. Den 'twas little honey an' lots 'lasses on bread. 'Twas good rations 'cause all de kids am fat lak little pigs. Ise can shut my eyes now an' see all dem younguns a-sattin' 'round de big pans wid de wooden spoons, eatin' potliquor an' co'nbread.

De cullud fo'ks on de marster's place had it hard. Dey have to wo'k early an' late. Ever'body has de task laid out fo' dem, an' dat deys have to do if it tooks dem all day an' night. Many's de time de fo'ks have to wo'k all night. 'Twas de whuppin's if dey fails.

De marster am a sweet, fine man. 'Twas his wife an' de overseer dat am tough. Dat womens had no mercy. She am a devil. Gosh fo' Mighty!, how Ise hates her. Youse see dem long ears Ise have? Well, dat's f'om de pullin' deys gits f'om her. Ise am wo'kin' 'round de house, keepin' flies off de fo'ks, gittin' wautah [water] and sich [such]. Fo' ever'thin' she don't lak [like], 'twas a ear-pullin' Ise gits. 'Twas pull, pull, an' some mo' pull ever'time she comes neah me.

She gives de ordah to de overseer dat so much must be done. She says, "Ise want so-an'-so many pairs of shoes made by sich-an'-sich time." It bettah be made if de wo'kers wants to keep f'om gittin' whupped. Yas, sar, dey makes all de shoes right dere. 'Twas my pappy's wo'k. Mammy wo'ked in de weavin' room. Many nights, yous could heah de bump, bump of de loom w'en mammy am wo'kin' to finish de task.

Sho', 'twas a busy place. 'Twas lak a town wid de diffe'nt businesses. Thar am de blacksmith shop, shoe shop, carpenter shop, de milk house, de marster had 'bout 100 milk cows, de weavin' room, de gin, an' de feed mill. Did yous ever see a hoss-powah [horse-powered] machine? Well, 'tis fixed wid long sweeps, an' dey goes 'round an' 'round. Dat-a-way [In that way], de powah fo' to run de gin an' grind de grist am made.

De missy knows ever'thing dat am gwine [going] on. She have de spies 'mong de cullud fo'ks. She tries to git me to report to her, but she finds Ise not 'pendable fo' sich, den stops. Once, she sends me to de sewin' room to see if de womens am wo'kin'. Some of dem am, an' some of dem ain't. W'en Ise returns, Ise says, "Deys all wo'kin'." Yous see, Ise raised by my mammy to tell nothin' Ise sees. Dat means to mind my own business.

Now, 'bout de whuppin's. Dey sometimes ties de nigger to a log an' den lash wid de whup. If de lash cuts de skin, den salt am put in de cut. De marster says de salt am fo' to p'otect de cut, but Ise see de squirmin' dat it causes. If deys have human feelin', 'twould be something else dat am use fo' to p'otect de cuts.

If someone asks 'bout de good times weuns have, jus' tell dem dat 'twarn't much. Weuns not 'lowed to go to church. Once in awhile during' de wintah, de marster would 'lows de party. Weuns had couple fiddles fo' de music.

Do weuns have de weddin's? White man, yous knows bettah dan dat. Dem times, de cullud fo'ks am jus' put together. 'Twas as de marster says. Him says, "Jim an' Nancy, yous go live together", and w'en de ordah am given, it bettah be done lak given. Dey thinks nothin' on de plantation 'bout de feelin's of de womens. No, sar, thar warn't no 'spect fo' de womens. De overseer an' tudder white mens tooks 'vantage of de womens lak dey wants to. De women bettah not make any fuss 'bout sich. If she does, 'twas a whuppin' fo' her. Ise sho' thank de Lawd surrendah [with freedom at the end of the Civil War] comes befo' Ise old 'nough to have to stand fo' sich. Yas, sar, surrendah saves dis nigger f'om sich.

Ise don't 'membahs much 'bout de wah days. De wautah on my brain hurts my 'membrance. Befo' Ise have de wautah, Ise could 'membahs mo'. Ise 'membahs Earl an' Jim, dat am de marster's sons. Dey goes to wah, an' never comes back 'cause both am killed.

Ise have de good 'collection w'en de wah am over, an' de sojers [soldiers] comes home. 'Twas thousands passed weuns's place. 'Twas as far as yous could see down de road. Dey am marchin' home f'om de wah. Some of dem camps neah de marster's place one night, an' some gits sick. Marster brings two of dem to de house fo' to doctah dem.

W'en weuns am put free [freed], de marster calls weuns to de quatahs. Ise never see so many cullud fo'ks in one crowd. De yard am full. Deys fixed a table. Marster stands on dat, an' made a talk to weuns. He tells weuns dat weuns am free, an' calls all de grown fo'ks, one by one, an' gives dem de statement 'bout de age [tells them their ages] an' sich. He tells dem dey could wo'k land on half [sharecrop], or wo'k fo' wages if dey wants to stay. He 'vised dem to stay awhile so deys could git a foothold, an' larn how to do.

Thar am lots dat stayed, an' some dat goes 'way. My fo'ks stayed fo' 'bout fouah yeahs [four years]. Father wo'ked land on shares 'til he gits a foothold, an' den buys a piece of land 'bout five miles f'om thar.

De land father buys ain't cleared, an' 'twarn't any buildin's on it, so weuns all pitches in an' fixed a cabin. Was weuns proud? Was weuns proud? Ise says weuns was w'en de cabin was done. Thar 'twas, our own home to do as weuns please after bein' slaves. Dat am sho' a good feelin'. After de cabin am built, weuns pitches in an' clears de land. 'Twarn't long 'til weuns am fixed to put in a crop. Weuns wo'ked lak beavers puttin' de crop in, an' 'tending to it. Weuns watched it grow lak 'twas a little chil' 'cause it all b'longed to weuns. 'Twas ours.

Ise de youngest, 'bout 12 yeahs old den. Ise tooks care of de house while mammy wo'ks wid de udders doin' de outside wo'k. My fo'ks stays thar 'til dey dies. Ise don't know what comes of de place, 'cause Ise left after Ise mai'ied [married]. Ise mai'ied de next yeah after weuns moved. Sho', dat am right. Ise jus' 13 yeahs old w'en Ise mai'ied de fust time. Ise mai'ied to Boss Powers. Weuns lives on rented land 'bout five miles f'om my fo'ks. Weuns lives together six yeahs, an' had three chilluns befo' he dies. 'Bout two yeahs later, Ise mai'ied Henry Ruffins. He died 26 yeahs ago. Ise have three chilluns by Ruffins. One am livin' in California, an' tudder two lives heah. Dey am de ones Ise lives wid now.

Sho', my name am Powers. Ise never tooks de name of Ruffins 'cause Ise dearly loved Powers. Co'se, Ise loved Ruffins, but Ise loved Powers so Ise can't stand to give up de name. Powers made a will, an' he has wrote on de paper "To my beloved wife, Ise gives all Ise have."

Warn't dat sweet of him? Well, Ise loved him, oh, so much, Ise could not give up his name. Dat's why Ise keeps it.

Ise come heah to Fort Worth to live after my second husband dies. Co'se, Ise wo'ked. Ise do housewo'k 'til few yeahs ago. Now, Ise gits $12.00 pension ever' month. Dat helps me to git by, an' Ise sho' needs it. Wid dis brain wautah, Ise sho' need it.

Now, 'bout de Klux [Ku Klux Klan], dem am devils. Ise don't have any fuss wid dem myself, but Ise knows tudder fo'ks dat does. Weuns never sleeps in de house after de Klux gits so bad. [This occurs after freedom.] 'Twas so bad, all de cullud fo'ks 'round thar sleeps out in de woods, or in ditches an' sich. Dey hides out ever'whar soon's [as soon as] dark comes, 'cause de Klux always comes in de dark time. Dey whups de cullud fo'ks fo' nothin', jus' fo' de fun dey gits outer it. Dat's de kind of fo'ks de Klux whar [were]. 'Twas fun fo' dem to injure fo'ks. Dey burn some houses an' destroyed property. Twice deys hung cullud fo'ks up by de thumbs. After awhile, de sojers [federal government soldiers] comes an' puts a stop to it.

Ise can't think of anymo' to tell. Dis wautah on my brain makes it hard fo' me to think. Ise never votes. 'Twas foolishment to ask dis old cullud person to does sich. Why does Ise wants to bother wid sich? De Lawd am gwine to took care of sich, an' Ise jus' leave it wid Him. De Lawd tooks care of slavery widout dem votin', an' Him will lead de way now fo' de cullud fo'ks.

CARTER J. JACKSON

Carter J. Jackson, age 85, at the time of interview

If yous wants to know 'bout slavery time, it was hell. I's born in Montgomery, over yonder in Alabama. My pappy named Charles and come from Florida and mammy named Charlotte and her from Tennessee. They was sold to Parson Rogers and brung to Alabama by him. I had seven brothers call Frank and Benjamin and Richardson and Anderson and Miles, Emanuel and Gill, and three sisters call Milanda, Evaline and Sallie, but I don't know if any of 'em are livin' now.

Parson Rogers come to Texas in '63 and brung 'bout 42 slaves. My first work was to tote water in the field. Parson lived in a good, big frame house. The niggers lived in log houses what had dirt floors and chimneys. Our bunks had rope slats and grass mattress. I sho' wish I could have cotch myself sleepin' on a feather bed them days. I wouldn't woke up 'til Kingdom Come.

We et [ate] vegetables and meat and ashcake. You could knock you mammy in the head, eatin' that ashcake bread. [Slang: "You could knock..." meaning the ashcake was extraordinarily good to eat.] I ain't been fit since. [Meaning, I haven't enjoyed anything as much as that since.] We had hominy [a corn product] cooked in the fireplace in big pots that ain't bad [was delicious] to talk 'bout. Deer was thick them days and we sot up sharp stobs [stakes] inside the pea field. Them young bucks jumps over the fence and stabs themselves. That the only way to cotch [catch] them 'cause they so wild you couldn't git a fair shot with a rifle.

Massa Rogers had a 300 acre plantation and 200 in cultivation. He had a overseer and Steve O'Neal was the nigger driver. The horn to git up blowed 'bout four o'clock and if we didn't fall out right now [get to the fields right away], the overseer was in after us. He tied us up every which way and whip us. At night, he walk the quarters to keep us from runnin' 'round. On Sunday mornin', the overseer come 'round to each nigger cabin with a big sack of shorts [food rations] and give us 'nough to make bread for one day.

I used to steal some chickens 'cause we didn't have 'nough to eat. I don' think I done wrong 'cause the place was full of 'em. We sho' earned what we et. I'd go up to the Big House to make fires. Lots of times I seed the mantel board lined with greenbacks, 'tween mantel and wall. I's snitched many a $50.00 bill, but it 'federate [Confederate] money.

Me and four of her chillen standin' by when mammy's sold for $500.00. Cryin' didn't stop 'em from sellin' our mammy 'way from us.

I 'member the War was tough. I went 'long with young Massa Dick when he went to the War to wait on him. I's standin' clost by when he was kilt [killed] under a big tree in Pittsburg. 'Fore he die, he ask Wes Tatum, one the neighbor boys from home, to take care of me and return me to Massa George.

I worked on for Massa Rogers four year after that, jus' like in slavery time. One day he call us and say we can go or stay. So I goes with my pappy and lives with him 'til 1871. Then I marries and works on the railroad when it's builded from Longview to Big Sandy, 'bout 1872. I works there sev'ral years and I raises seven chillen. After I quits the railroad, I works wherever I can, on farms or in town.

SILAS JACKSON

I was born at or near Ashbie's Gap in Virginia, either in the year of 1846 or 47, I do not know which, but I will say I am 90 years of age. My father's name was Sling and mother's Sarah Louis. They were purchased by my master from a slave trader in Richmond, Virginia. My father was a man of large stature and my mother was tall and stately. They originally came from the Eastern Shore of Maryland, I think from the Legg estate. Beyond that, I do not know. I had three brothers and two sisters. My brothers older than I, and my sisters younger. Their names were Silas, Carter, Rap or Raymond, I do not remember. My sisters were Jane and Susie, both of whom are living in Virginia now. Only one I have ever seen and he came north with General Sherman. He died in 1926. He was a Baptist minister like myself.

The only things I know about my grandparents were: My grandfather ran away through the aid of Harriet Tubman and went to Philadelphia, and saved $350 and purchased my grandmother through the aid of a Quaker or an Episcopal minister, I do not know. I have on several occasions tried to trace this part of my family's past history, but without success.

I was a large boy for my age. When I was nine years of age, my task began and continued until 1864. You see, I saw, and I was a slave.

In Virginia where I was, they raised tobacco, wheat, corn and farm products. I have had a taste of all the work on the farm, besides of digging and clearing up new ground to increase the acreage to the farm. We all had task work to do — men, woman, and boys. We began work on Monday and worked until Saturday. That day we were allowed to work for ourselves and to garden or to do extra work. When we could get work, or work on someone else's place, we got a pass [pass, see page 7] from the overseer to go off the plantation, but to be back by nine o'clock on Saturday night or when cabin inspection was made. Sometime we could earn as much as 50 cents a day, which we used to buy cakes, candies or clothes.

On Saturday each slave was given 10 pounds of cornmeal, a quart of blackstrap [molasses], 5 pounds of fatback [pork fat], 3 pounds of flour, and vegetables, all of which were raised on the farm. All of the slaves hunted, or those who wanted, hunted rabbits, opossums or fished. These were our choice foods as we did not get anything special from the overseer. Our food was cooked by our mothers or sisters and, for those who were not married, by the old women and men assigned for that work.

Each family was given 3 acres to raise their chickens or vegetables. If a man raised his own food, he was given $10.00 at Christmas time extra, besides his presents.

In the summer or when warm weather came, each slave was given something: the women, linsey goods or gingham clothes; the men overalls, muslin shirts, top and underclothes, two pair of shoes, and a straw hat to work in. In cold weather, we wore woolen clothes, all made at the sewing cabin.

My master was named Tom Ashbie, a meaner man was never born in Virginia — brutal, wicked and hard. He always carried a cowhide [whip] with him. If he saw anyone doing something that did not suit his taste, he would have the slave tied to a tree, man or woman, and then would cowhide the victim until he got tired, or sometimes the slave would faint.

The Ashbie's home was a large stone mansion with a porch on three sides, wide halls in the center, up and down stairs, numerous rooms and a stone kitchen built on the back connected with dining room.

Mrs. Ashbie was kind and lovely to her slaves when Mr. Ashbie was out. The Ashbies did not have any children of their own, but they had boys and girls of his own sister and they were much like him. They had maids or private waiters for the young men if they wanted them.

I have heard it said by people in authority, Tom Ashbie owned 9,000 acres of farm land besides of wood land. He was a large slaveowner having more than 100 slaves on his farm. They were awakened by blowing of the horn before sunrise by the overseer, started to work at sunrise and worked all day to sundown, with not time to go to the cabin for dinner [lunch]. You carried your dinner with you. The slaves were driven at top speed and whipped at the snap of the finger by the overseers. We had four overseers on the farm, all hired white men. I have seen men beaten until they dropped in their tracks or knocked over by clubs, women stripped down to their waist and cowhided.

I have heard it said that Tom Ashbie's father went to one of the cabins late at night. The slaves were having a secret prayer meeting. He heard one slave ask God to change the heart of his master and deliver him from slavery so that he may enjoy freedom. Before the next day, the man disappeared, no one ever seeing him again. But after that, down in the swamp at certain times of the moon, you could hear the man who prayed in the cabin praying. When old man Ashbie died, just before he died, he told the white Baptist minister that he had killed Zeck for praying and that he was going to Hell.

There was a stone building on the farm. It is there today [in 1937]. I saw it this summer while visiting in Virginia. The old jail, it is now used as a garage. Downstairs there were two rooms, one where some of the whipping was done, and the other used by the overseer. Upstairs was used for women and girls. The iron bars have corroded, but you can see where they were. I have never seen slaves sold on the farm, but I have seen them taken away, and brought there. Several times I have seen slaves chained taken away and chained when they came.

No one on the place was taught to read or write. On Sunday, the slaves who wanted to worship would gather at one of the large cabins with one of the overseers present and have their church. After which the overseer would talk. When communion was given, the overseer was paid for staying there with half of the collection taken up. Sometime he would get 25¢. No one could read the Bible. Sandy Jasper, Mr. Ashbie's coachman was the preacher. He would go to the white Baptist church on Sunday with [the slaveowner's] family and would be better informed because he heard the white preacher.

Twice each year, after harvest and after New Year's, the slaves would have their protracted meeting or their revival. After each closing, they would baptize in the creek. Sometimes in the winter, they would break the ice singing *Going to the Water* or some other hymn of that nature. And at each funeral, the Ashbies would attend the service conducted in the cabin where the deceased was, from there taken to the slave graveyard. A lot [was] dedicated for that purpose, situated about 3/4 of a mile from the cabins near a hill.

There were a number of slaves on our plantation who ran away. Some were captured and sold to a Georgia trader; others who were never captured. To intimidate the slaves, the overseers were connected with the patrollers, not only to watch our slaves, but sometimes for the rewards for other slaves who had run away from other plantations. This feature caused a great deal of trouble between whites and blacks. In 1858, two men were murdered near Warrenton on the road by colored people. It was never known whether by free people or slaves.

When work was done, the slaves retired to their cabins. Some played games, others cooked or rested or did what they wanted. We did not work on Saturdays unless harvest times, then Saturdays were days of work. At other times on Saturdays, you were at leisure to do what you wanted. On Christmas Day, Mr. Ashbie would call all the slaves together, give them presents, money, after which they spent the day as they liked. On New Year's Day, we all were scared. That was the time for selling, buying, and trading slaves. We did not know who was to go or come.

I do not remember of playing any particular game. My sport was fishing. You see, I do not believe in ghost stories or voodooism, I have nothing to say. We boys used to take horns of a dead cow or bull, cut the end off of it. We could blow it, some having different notes. We could tell who was blowing and from what plantation.

When a slave took sick, she or he would have to depend on herbs, salves or other remedies prepared by someone who knew the medicinal value. When a valuable hand took sick, one of the overseers would go to Upper Ville for a doctor.

WILLIAM MATHEWS
(See page 60 for full life story):
De quarters is back of de Big House and didn't have no floors. Dey sot plumb on de ground and build like a hawg [hog] pen.

ANTHONY CHRISTOPHER:
We has good brick quarters, too, yes suh, an' wood floors 'stead of jes' being on de ground like some had.

LOUISE MATHEWS

Louise Mathews at time of interview

Sho' [Sure], Ise 'membahs slavery times 'cause Ise 83 yeahs old now. Ise 11 yeahs old w'en de breakup [emancipation of the slaves] comes. Ise bo'n in Shelby County, Texas, on the farm dat b'longs to Marster Robert Turner. Ever'body calls him Judge Turner. He was a Baptist preacher, an' run a small farm an' a gen'ral store, too. Thar am seven fam'lies of slaves on Marster's place. 'Twas my mother, she had nine chilluns, an' six tudder fam'lies. Ise don't know nothin' 'bout my father, 'cept Ise told he am in Virginia. W'en Ise old 'nough to 'membahs, mother am mai'ied to Tom Hooper. He am owned by Marster Jack Hooper dat owns a farm fouah [four] miles f'om Marster's place. Marster Turner am de preacherman dat mai'ied dem.

Mostest de cullud fo'ks jus' lives together by 'greement in slavery time, but 'twas diffe'nt on Marster's place. De marster says de ce'emony

44

fo' de mai'iage. He gits de couple together an' says, "Do youse tooks dis man to be youse husband, and do youse tooks dis womens to be youse wife? What de Lawd jines together, let no man put asunder." Youse see, 'twas jus' lak de white fo'ks does w'en dey mai'ies.

Weuns lives in cabins built f'om logs. Dey am double cabins, an' mostest of dem have two fam'lies livin' in dem. Dey am jus' lak all tudder cabins in slavery time wid dirt flooah [floor], no windahs, jus' [square] holes in de wall. Weuns sleeps in bunks wid straw ticks [mattresses]. De cabins all had a fireplace, but deys used fo' heat mostly, in de wintertime. De cookin' am done at one place. 'Twas my gran'mammy dat done de cookin' fo' de wo'kers. Now, 'twas 'lowed to cook in de cabins fo' special doin's, lak if thar am a visitor. My mammy always cooks in her cabin w'en my stepfather comes to see weuns. He comes ever' Wednesday an' Saturday night, an' den she cooks de meal fo' weuns. Sho', Marster 'lows dat, an' my stepfather had a good marster, too.

Ise gwine tell youse how my stepfather's marster does wid most of his slaves. He 'lows dem one acre of land an' gives dem time to wo'k it. All dey makes on de acre am given to de nigger. Father always plants his acre in cotton. W'en Marster Hooper takes his cotton to town, father's cotton goes, too, an' what it brings am given to father. Well, dat-a-way [in that way], father can buy things fo' himself, so he has his own hoss [horse] an' saddle, an' he brings us good things to eat our marster don't furnish, sich as de coffee an' tea. Co'se, he brings us candy sometimes, an' things to play wid. 'Twas green coffee dat father always brings, an' mammy would roast, grind it an' make coffee fo' allus w'en her man comes to visit weuns.

Marster Turner always gives weuns good rations. Dat-a-way, he am awful good, but what father brings am jus' extra. Father sho' does well wid his acre of land. Co'se he gits all his rations an' clothes f'om his marster jus' lak all slaves does, so he could save all he makes. Well, w'en surrendah comes, he had over $500.00 saved, an' 'twarn't [it was not] worth a cent. Ise 'membahs how he called allus chilluns together an' says, "Heah [Here] am lots of money youse can have." Weuns tooks it an' plays store wid it. 'Twas Confederate money am de reason 'twarn't no good.

Weuns sho' lives good on Marster Turner's place. Co'se, dey raises ever'thing dey uses in dem days, an' 'twas plenty of it. Lots of co'n [corn], cane, veg'tables, 'sides de cotton. 'Twas plenty of hawgs

[hogs] fo' de meat, cows fo' de milk an' buttah, chickens fo' chicken meat an' eggs, an' bees fo' de honey. So, de rations am plenty of good food. No, sar, weuns am never hongry. De clothes weuns have am made on de marster's place on his own loom. Weuns always had plenty linsey-woolsey clothes.

Let me tell youse how de younguns am cared fo'. Dey's given special care by de marster. De food am lots of clabber milk, co'nbread, potliquor [the liquid from cooked greens] wid co'nbread crumbled up in it. 'Twas good food fo' sho' 'cause dey's all fat an' healthy. De marster had a special medicine fo' weuns dat he makes. Youse see, he runs a store an' sells whiskey.

Yas, sar, he am a preacherman, farmer, an' a saloonkeeper. Well, now Ise tells youse how he makes de medicine. He tooks some whiskey an' puts cherry bark in it, also de rust off nails an' iron. Dat am de medicine weuns have to took. Well, it must be good 'cause 'twarn't much sickness, an' weuns am all fat an' sassy. Gosh fo' Mighty! How Ise hates to took dat medicine! Bittahs [Bitters] am what 'twas called, an' 'twas bittah fo' sho'. De marster 'tends to givin' de bittahs himself. He am pa'ticulah 'bout de younguns, how dey's fed an' ever'thing. Ise often heah him says to Anne, dat am de cullud womens as tooks care of de chilluns, "Anne, tooks good care of de younguns 'cause de old ones gwine [going] to play out sometime an' Ise wants de younguns to grow to be strong niggers."

Yas, sar, ever'thing am lovely wid weuns on dat plantation. 'Twarn't no whuppin's dat Ise knows of. All de cullud fo'ks am satisfied wid what de marster gives dem, an' tries hard to please him, an' he am satisfied wid de wo'kers so 'twarn't no trouble.

'Twas only one runawayer, an' he runs back to de marster's farm 'stead of 'way f'om him. 'Twas dis-a-way: Marster hires him out [rents him] to a man named Murphy. Well, Murphy wo'ks de man all night an' day, an' den ain't satisfied so de cullud fellow runs off an' comes home. Sho', de marster often hires out a slave if dey can spare one an' some tudder marster am short of help. De marster would hire one out fo' so much [a certain amount of money] a day. Well, w'en John shows up at home, Marster asks him why he came home. John told him how 'twas he am wo'ked an' Marster says he did him jus' right. He says, "Ise don't hire youse out to be worked to death." Dat same day, Murphy shows up an' wants to git John, but Marster says, "No, sar! Ise knows

John am a good wo'ker an' w'en he says he am overwo'ked, Ise knows he am overwo'ked." Murphy am purtty riled [very angry] 'bout it but had to go off widout John.

Marster Turner am very reasonable 'bout de wo'k. He want a good day's wo'k, an' all de cullud fo'ks gives it to him. Weuns had Saturday afternoons off an', co'se, Sundays, too. Weuns does de washin' an' sich wo'k as weuns wants to do fo' ourselves on Saturdays, den weuns could go to parties at night. De marster gives weuns a pass [permission slip to leave the plantation] ever' Saturday night if weuns wanted it. Weuns had to have de pass 'cause de patterollers [patrollers] am watchin' fo' de cullud fo'ks as don't have de pass. Weuns have singin' an' dancin' at de parties. De dancin' am quadrilles an' de music am fiddles an' banjoes.

Weuns all goes to chu'ch on Sundays. Co'se, de marster am de preacher. He preached to his white fo'ks in de evenin'. 'Twas cullud fo'ks as comes f'om all 'round tudder plantations to weuns chu'ch. Dat am de way weuns lives on de marster's place, an' 'twas de same on stepfather's place.

Ever'thing am changed w'en surrendah comes. Well does Ise 'membahs de day Marster Turner come out in de yard of de cullud qua'tahs, an' calls allus 'round him. Ise can see him now, lak Ise watched him comin' to de yard wid his hands clasped 'hind him an' his head bowed, walkin' slowly. W'en he gits to de yard, he tells my uncle to call allus to him. W'en weuns gits together, he starts talkin' slowly an' says, "Fo'ks," Ise 'membahs de words well, "Ise laks ever' one of youse. Youse have been faithful but Ise have to give youse up. Ise hates to do it, not 'cause Ise don't want to free youse, but 'cause Ise don't want to lose youse all. Ise guess 'tis de bestest fo' you, an' for dat, Ise glad. Youse, f'om dis moment, am free fo'ks jus' lak Ise am or tudder white fo'ks." Den he stops talkin' fo' a little bit, an' weuns could see tears in his eyes. W'en he talks 'gain, he says, "Ise wants youse all to stay on de farm an' weuns can wo'k de land on shares." [For more about shares, see page 7.]

Most de cullud fo'ks leaves de place an' went back to de fo'ks de marster buys dem f'om. Some went to Dawg Robinson, some to Maddox, an' some to Reeves. Co'se, my mammy tooks weuns chilluns an' goes to Hooper's place whar father am. Weuns lives thar on de Hooper place fo' seven yeahs after de breakup. Weuns comes to Fort

Worth in 1872, an' 'twas right whar weuns am livin' now. 'Twarn't settled den. Weuns farmed land whar all de houses am now in dis section.

Reason father moves f'om Shelby County am 'cause de Ku Klux Klan [see page 8] gits so bad pesterin' de niggers. De men fo'ks am 'fraid to sleep in de house, an' would go to ravines, de woods, an' sich whar dey could hide. Weuns never had any trouble on de marster's place, but am 'fraid to go any place. 'Twas two cullud mens shot neah weuns. De Klux comes to de house an' de cullud fellows tries to fit [fight] dem off. 'Cause de cullud fellows fits them, de Klux shoots dem.

Father git 'gusted after dat an' says, " 'Tis time to move f'om sich country." After weuns comes heah, Ise gits mai'ied de fust time. 'Twas in 1874 an' Ise 20 yeahs old. 'Twas to Henry Daggett. He b'long to Marster Daggett befo' surrendah an' he lives on de Daggett Ranch. He dies in 1884. 'Bout a yeah after dat, Ise mai'ied to Jim Byers, an' weuns sep'rated de next yeah. Dat man was lazy an' no 'count. Ise jus' keeps fustin' wid him an' 'sistin' dat he go to wo'k. W'en he see dat Ise means it, he leaves an' 'twas de last Ise ever sees of him. 'Twas on a Christmas Day in de mo'nin', an' 'twas de only Christmas present he ever made me. He am what am called de "Buck Passer". Ise did washin' an' ironin', an' he passes de bucks Ise made away. Ise mai'ies Bill Mathews de next yeah. He makes weuns livin' at common labor, am 'dustrious, an' tooks good care of his fam'ly.

Ise de mother of seven chilluns. 'Twas three by Henry Daggett, one by Jim Byers, an' three by Bill Mathews. He died on May 15, dis yeah. Jus' fouah of my chilluns am still livin', an' deys all heah in Fort Worth.

Votin'? Well, Ise only voted once 'bout fouah yeahs ago. Ise jus' don't care 'bout it 'cause 'tis too much fustin' 'round. Bill Mathews always voted in de gen'ral 'lection, an' he always voted de Lincoln Ticket.

Yas, sar, my health am good. Ise gits 'round an' does my housewo'k. Ise feels good but Ise knows 'twon't be long 'til Ise goes to de restin' place de Lawd has fo' weuns. Now, if youse wants to know anymo', youse go to my sis', Scott Hooper. She am 81 yeahs old, an' lives in de next block yonder way. She m'ybe 'membahs somethin' Ise done left out.

JAMES V. DEANE

My name is James V. Deane, son of John and Jane Deane, born at Goose Bay in Charles County [Maryland], May 20, 1850. My mother was the daughter of Vincent Harrison. I do not know about my father's people. I have two sisters, both of whom are living, Sarah and Elizabeth Ford.

I was born in a log cabin, a typical Charles County log cabin, at Goose Bay on the Potomac River. The plantation on which I was born fronted more than three miles on the river. The cabin had two rooms, one up and one down, very large with two windows, one in each room. There were no porches. Over the door was a wide board to keep the rain and snow from beating over the top of the door, with a large log chimney on the outside, plastered between the logs, in which was a fireplace with an open grate to cook on and to put logs on the fire to heat.

We slept on a homemade bedstead, on which was a straw mattress and upon that was a feather mattress, on which we used quilts made by mother to cover.

As a slave, I worked on the farm with other small boys thinning corn, watching watermelon patches, and later I worked in wheat and tobacco fields. The slaves never had nor earned any cash money.

Our food was very plain, such as fat hog meat, fish and vegetables raised on the farm and cornbread made up with salt and water.

Yes, I have hunted opossums and 'coons [raccoons]. The last time I went 'coon hunting, we treed something. It fell out of the tree [and] everybody took to their heels, white and colored. The white men outran the colored hunter leading the gang. I never went hunting afterwards.

My choice food was fish and crabs cooked in all styles by mother. You have asked about gardens. Yes, some slaves had small garden patches which they worked by moonlight.

As for clothes, we all wore homemade clothes, the material woven on the looms in the clothes house. In the winter, we had woolen clothes, and in summer, our clothes were made from cast-off clothes and Kentucky jeans. Our shoes were brogans with brass tips. On Sunday, we fed the stock, after which we did what we wanted.

I have seen many slave weddings, the master holding a broom handle, the groom jumping over it as a part of the wedding ceremony.

When a slave married someone from another plantation, the master of the wife owned all the children. For the wedding, the groom wore ordinary clothes. Sometimes you could not tell the original outfit for the patches and sometimes Kentucky jeans. The bride's trousseau: she would wear the cast-off clothes of the mistress or, at other times, the clothes made by other slaves.

It is said our plantation contained 10,000 acres. We had a large number of slaves. I do not know the number. Our work was hard, from sunup to sundown. The slaves were not whipped.

There was only one slave ever sold from the plantation. She was my aunt. The mistress slapped her one day. She struck her back. She was sold and taken south. We never saw or heard of her afterwards.

We went to the white Methodist church with a slave gallery, only white preachers. We sang with the white people. The Methodists were christened and the Baptist were baptized. I have seen many colored funerals with no service. A graveyard [was] on the place. [There was] only a wooden post to show where you were buried.

None of the slaves ran away. I have seen and heard many patrollers, but they never whipped any of Mason's slaves. The method of conveying news [was] you tell me and I tell you, but be careful, no troubles between whites and blacks.

After work was done, the slaves would smoke, sing, tell ghost stories and tales, dances, music, homemade fiddles. Saturday was a work day like any other day. We had all legal holidays. Christmas morning, we went to the Big House and got presents and had a big time all day.

At cornshucking, all the slaves from the other plantations would come to the barn. The fiddler would sit on top of the highest barrel of corn and play all kinds of songs. [We had] a barrel of cider [and a] jug of whiskey [with] one man to dish out a drink of liquor each hour, cider when wanted. We had supper [lunch] at twelve, roast pig for everybody, applesauce, hominy [a corn product], and cornbread. We went back to shucking. The carts from the other farms would be there to haul it to the corn crib. [The] dance would start after the corn was stored. We danced until daybreak.

The only games we played were marbles, mumble pegs [mumblety-peg], and ring plays. We sang London Bridge.

When we wanted to meet at night, we had an old conk [shell]. We blew that. We all would meet on the bank of the Potomac River and sing

50

across the river to the slaves in Virginia, and they would sing back to us.

Some people say there are no ghosts, but I saw one and I am satisfied. I saw an old lady who was dead. She was only five feet from me. I met her face to face. She was a white woman. I knew her. I liked to tore [almost tore] the door off the hinges getting away.

My master's name was Thomas Mason. He was a man of weak mental disposition. His mother managed the affairs. He was kind. Mrs. Mason had a good disposition. She never permitted the slaves to be punished. The main house was very large with porches on three sides. No children, no overseer.

The poor white people in Charles County were worse off than the slaves because they could not get any work to do. On the plantation, the slaves did all the work.

Some time ago, you asked did I ever see slaves sold. I have seen slaves tied behind buggies going to Washington [DC] and some to Baltimore [MD].

No one was taught to read. We were taught the Lord's Prayer and catechism.

When the slaves took sick, Dr. Henry Mudd, the one who gave Booth first aid [John Wilkes Booth?, President Abraham Lincoln's assassin who became injured], was our doctor. The slaves had herbs of their own and made their own salves. The only charms that were worn were made out of bones.

Stone slave quarters in Maryland

ADELINE MARSHALL

Yes, suh, Adeline Marshall am my name all right, but folks 'round here jes' calls me "Grandma".

Lawd, have mercy. I's been in dis here land too long, too long, and jes' ain't no 'count no more for nothin'. I got mis'ries in my bones and jes' look at what I's got on my feet! Dem's jes' rags, dat's all, rags. Can't wear nothin' else on 'em, dey hurts so. Dat's what de red russet shoes what we wears in slave times done — jes' pizen [poison] de feets.

Lawd, Lawd, dat sho' bad times. Black folks jes' raise up like cattle in de stable. Only Cap'n Brevard — he what own me — treats he hosses and cattle better'n he do he niggers.

Don't know nothin' 'bout myself 'cept on Cap'n Brevard's place down on Oyster Creek. He has de plantation dere, what de only place I knows 'til I's freedomed. He says I's a South Car'lina nigger what he bought back dere and brung to Texas when I jes' a baby. I reckon [guess] it de truth 'cause I ain't never knowed no mama or papa, neither one.

Cap'n he a bad man and he drivers hard, too, all de time whippin' and stroppin' de niggers to make dem work harder. Didn't make no difference to Cap'n how little you is, you goes out to de field 'mos' soon's [almost as soon as] you can walk. De drivers don't use de bullwhip on de little niggers [the slave children], but dey plays [they hit with] de switch on us what sting de hide plenty. Sometimes dey puts a nigger in de stocks and leaves dem two or three days, don't give dem nothin' to eat or a drink of water, jes' leaves dem 'til dey 'mos' dead. Does dey die [If they do die], jes' put dem in a box and dig a hole out back of de hoss [horse] lot and dump dem in and cover up. Ain't no preachin service or nothin', but de poor nigger out he mis'ry, dat's all.

Old Cap'n jes' hard on he niggers. I 'member one time dey strops [whipped with a leather strap] old Beans what's so old he can't work good no more. In de mornin', dey finds him hangin' from a tree back of de quarters. He done hang himself to 'scape he mis'ry!

We works every day 'cept Sunday and has to do our washin' den. Does anybody git sick weekdays, he has to work Sunday to make it up.

When we comes in at night, we has to go right to bed. Dey don't 'low no light in de quarters and you better be in bed if you don't want a whippin'.

We gits a plain cotton slip [slip, meaning a dress, not underwear] with a string 'round de neck, de stuff dey makes pickin' sacks of. Summer or winter, dat all we gits to wear.

Old Cap'n have a big house, but I jes' see it from de quarters 'cause we wasn't 'lowed to go up in de yard. I hear say he don't have no wife, but a black woman what stays at de house. Dat de reason so many "no nation" niggers 'round. Some calls dem "bright" niggers, but I calls dem "no nation" 'cause dat what dey is, ain't all black or all white, but mix [mulattoes]. Dat comes from slave times.

I knows I's good [large] size when Old Cap'n calls us in and says we's free, but nobody tell me how old I is and I never found out. I knows some of us stays and works for somethin' to eat 'cause we didn't know no one and didn't have nowheres to go.

Den one day, Cap'n comes out in de field with 'nother man and pick me and four more what's workin' and say we's good workers. Dat was Mr. Jack Adams what have a place clost to Stafford's Run. He say if we wants to work on his place, he feed us and give quarters and pay us for workin'. Dat how come I leaves old Cap'n, and I ain't never see him or dat place where I's raise since. I reckon he so mean de debbil [devil] done got him in torment long time ago.

I works in de field for Mr. Jack and dat where Wes Marshall, what I marries, works, too. After we gits married, we gits a piece of ground and stays on de same place 'til Mr. Jack die and we come to Houston. Dat 'fore de 1900 storm.

I tells folks when dat storm comin'. I ain't 'lieve in no witch doin's, but some way I knows when dat storm comin'. Dey laughs at dis old nigger, but it come and dey looses hosses and cattle and chickens and houses.

I tells de truth jes' like it am, and I's had a hard time in de land. Why, in dis sinful town, dey don't do like de Good Book say. No, suh, dey don't. It say, "Love they neighbor" and folks don't love nobody but theyselves!

Jes' look at me! I's old with mis'ry and 'lone in de world. My husband and chillen done die long ago and leave me here, and I jes' go from house to house tryin' to find a place to stay. Dat why I prays Gawd to take me to his bosom, 'cause He de onlies' one I got to call on.

JENNY PROCTOR

Jenny Proctor at time of interview

I's hear tell of dem good slave days but I ain't nev'r seen no good times den. My mother's name wuz Lisa. When I wuz a very small chile, I hear dat driver goin' from cabin to cabin [in Alabama] as early as three o'clock in de mornin'. When he comes to our cabin, he say, "Lisa, Lisa, git up from dere and git dat breakfast." My mother she wuz a cook and I don't recollect nothin' 'bout my father. If I had any brothers or sistas, I didn' knows it.

We had ole ragged huts made out of poles and some of de cracks wuz chinked up wid mud and moss and some of dem wuzn't. We didn' have no good bed, jes' scaffolds nailed up to de wall out of poles and de ole ragged beddin' throwed on dem. Dat sho' wuz hard sleepin' but even dat feel good to our weary bones after dem long hard days' work in de field.

I tended to de chillun when I wuz a little gal and tried to clean de house jes' like Ole Miss tells me to. Den soon as I was 10 years ole, Ole Marster he say, "Git dis yere nigger to dat cotton patch." I recollects once when I wuz a-tryin' to clean de house like Ole Miss tell me, I finds a biscuit and I's so hungry I et [ate] it, 'cause we nev'r see sich a thing as a biscuit, only sometimes on Sunday mornin'. We jes' have co'nbraid [cornbread] and syrup and sometimes fat bacon. When I et dat biscuit and she comes in and say, "Whar dat biscuit?", I say, "Miss, I et it 'cause I's so hungry." Den she grab dat broom and start to beatin' me over de head wid it and callin' me low-down nigger. I guess I jes' clean lost my head 'cause I know'd better den to fight her if I knowed anythin' 'tall [at all]. But I start to fight her and de driver he comes in and he grabs me and starts beatin' me wid dat cat-o'-nine-tails [whip]. He beats me 'til I fall to de floor nearly dead. He cut my back all to pieces, den dey rubs salt in de cuts for mo' punishment. Lawd, Lawd, honey! Dem wuz awful days.

When Ole Marster come to de house, he say, "What you beat dat nigger like dat for?" And de driver tells him why and he say, "She can't work now for a week. She pay for several biscuits in dat time." He sho' wuz mad and tell Ole Miss she start de whole mess. I still got dem scars on my ole back right now, jes' like my grandmother have when she die and I's a-carryin' mine right on to de grave jes' like she did.

Our marster he wouldn' 'low us to go fishin'. He say dat too easy on a nigger and wouldn' 'low us to hunt none either, but sometime we slips off at night and ketch 'possums. When Ole Marster smells dem 'possums cookin' way in de night, he wraps up in a white sheet and gits in de chimney corner and scratch on de wall. When de man in de cabin goes to de door and say, "Who's dat?", he say, "Hit's [It is] me. What's ye cookin' in dere?" De man say, "I's cookin' 'possum." He say, "Cook him and bring me de hind quarters and you and de wife and de chillum eat de rest." We nev'r had no chance ter git any rabbits 'cept when we wuz a-clearin' and a-grubbin' de new grounds. Den we ketch some rabbits and if dey looks good to de white folks, dey takes dem and if dey say no good, de niggers git dem. We nev'r had no gardens. Sometimes de slaves git vegetables from the white folks' garden and sometimes dey didn'.

Money? Uh-um! [No!] We nev'r seen no money. Guess we'd a-bought sumpin' to eat wid it if we ev'r seen any. Fact is, we wouldn' a-knowed hardly how to bought anythin' 'cause we didn' know nothin' 'bout goin' to town.

Dey spinned de cloth what our clothes wuz made of and we had straight dresses or slips [slips were straight dresses, not underwear] made of lowel. Sometimes dey dye 'em wid sumac berries or sweet gum bark and sometimes dey didn'. On Sunday, dey make all de chillun change. What we wears 'til we gits our clothes washed wuz gunny sacks wid holes cut for our head and arms. We didn' have no shoes 'ceptin' some homemade moccasins and we didn' have dem 'til we wuz big chillun. De little chillun dey goes naked 'til dey wuz big enough to work. Dey wuz soon big enough though, 'cordin' to our marster. We had red flannel for winter underclothes. Ole Miss she say a sick nigger cost more den de flannel. Weddin's, uh-um! [no!] We jes' steps over de broom and we's married. Ha, ha, ha!

Ole marster he had a good house. De logs all hewed off smooth like and de cracks all fixed wid nice chinkin', plum [completely] 'spectable lookin' even to de plank floors. Dat wuz sumpin' [something]. He didn't have no big plantation but keeps 'bout 300 slaves in dem little huts wid dirt floors. I thinks he calls it four farms what he had.

Sometimes he would sell some of de slaves off of dat big auction block to de highest bidder when he could git enough for one. When he go to sell a slave, he feed dat one good for a few days. Den when he goes to put 'em up on the auction block, he takes a meat skin and greases all 'round dat nigger's mouth to make 'em look like dey been eatin' plenty meat and sich like, and wuz good and strong and able to work. Sometimes he sell de babes from de breas', and den again he sell de mothers from de babes, and de husbands and de wives, and so on. He wouldn't let 'em holler [cry loudly or scream] much when de folks be sold away. He say, "I have you whooped if you don't hush." Dey sho' loved deir [their own] six chillun though. Dey wouldn' want nobody buyin' dem.

We might a-done very well if de ole driver [slavedriver = overseer] hadn't been so mean. But de least little thing we do, he beat us for it and put big chains 'round our ankles and make us work wid dem on 'til de blood be cut out all 'round our ankles. Some of de marsters have what dey call stockades and puts deir heads and feet and arms through holes in a big board out in de hot sun. But our old driver he had a bullpen. Dat's only thing like a jail he had. When a slave do anythin' he didn' like, he takes 'em in dat bullpen and chains 'em down, face up to de sun and leaves 'em dere 'til dey nearly dies.

None of us wuz 'lowed to see a book or try to learn. Dey say we git smarter den dey wuz if we learn anythin', but we slips around and gits hold of that Webster's old blue back speller and we hides it 'til way in de night. Den we lights a little pine [knot] torch and studies dat spellin' book. We learn it, too. I can read some now and write a little, too.

Dey [There] wuzn't no church for de slaves but we goes to de white folks' arbor on Sunday evenin'. A white man he gits up dere to preach to de niggers. He say, "Now I takes my text, which is, nigger obey your marster and your mistress 'cause what you git from dem here in dis world am all you ev'r goin' to git, 'cause you jes' like de hogs and de other animals. When you dies, you ain't no more after you been throwed in dat hole." I guess we believed dat for awhile 'cause we didn' have no way findin' out different. We didn' see no Bibles.

Sometimes a slave would run away and jes' live wild in de woods but most times dey ketch 'em and beats 'em, den chains 'em down in de hot sun 'til dey nearly die. De only way any slaves on our farm ev'r goes anywhere wuz when de boss sends him to carry some news to another plantation or when we slips off way in de night. Sometimes after all de work wuz done, a bunch would have it made up [made up their minds = decided] to slip out down to de creek and dance. We sho' have fun when we do dat, most times on Sat'day night.

All de Christmas we had wuz Ole Marster would kill a hog and give us a piece of poak [pork]. We thought dat wuz sumpin'. De way Christmas lasted wuz 'cordin' to de big sweet gum back log what de slaves would cut and put in de fireplace. When dat burned out, de Christmas wuz over. So you know we all keeps a-lookin' de whole year 'roun' for de biggest sweet gum we could find. When we jes' couldn' find de sweet gum, we git oak, but it wouldn' last long enough, 'bout three days on average when we didn' have to work. Ole Marster he sho' pile on dem pineknots [to make the fire burn hotter on the yule log], gittin' dat Christmas over so we could git back to work.

We had a few little [children's] games we play, like "Peep, Squirrel, Peep," "You Can't Ketch Me," and sich like. We didn' know nothin' 'bout no New Year's Day or holidays 'cept Christmas.

We had some co'nshuckin's sometimes but de white folks gits de fun and de nigger gits de work. We didn' have no kind of cottonpickin's 'cept jes' pick our own cotton. I's can hear dem darkies now, goin to de cotton patch way 'fore day a-singin' "Peggy, Does You Love Me Now?" One ole man he sing:

"Sat'day night and Sunday, too
Young gals on my mind,
Monday mornin' way 'fore day
Ole Marster got me gwine.
Peggy, does you love me now?"

Den he whoops a sort of nigger holler, what nobody can do jes' like dem ole-time darkies. Den he goes:

" 'Possum up a 'simmon tree [persimmon, a fruit],
Rabbit on de groun'
Lawd, Lawd, 'possum
Shake dem 'simmons down.
Peggy, does you love me now?
Holler.
Rabbit up a gum stump
'Possum up a holler
Git him out, little boy
And I gives you half a dollar.
Peggy, does you love me now?
Holler."

We didn' have much lookin' after [much care] when we got sick. We had to take de worst stuff in de world fer medicine, jes' so it wuz cheap. Dat ole blue mass and bitter apple would keep us out all night. Sometimes he have de doctor when he thinks we goin' to die 'cause he say he ain't got ary [any] one to lose. Den dat calomel what dat doctor would give us would purty nigh [pretty near = almost] kill us. Den dey keeps all kinds of lead bullets and asafoetida balls 'roun' our necks and some carried a rabbit foot wid dem all de time to keep off evil of any kind.

Lawd, Lawd, honey! It seems impossible dat any of us ev'r lived to see dat day of freedom, but thank God we did.

When Ole Marster comes down in de cotton patch to tells us 'bout bein' free, he say, "I's hates to tell you but I's knows I's got to . You is free, jes' as free as me or anybody else what's white." We didn' hardly know what he mean. We jes' sort of huddle 'roun' together like skeered [scared] rabbits. But after we knowed what he mean, didn' many of us go 'cause we didn' know where to went. Ole Marster he say he give us de woods land and half of what we make on it. We could clear it and work it or starve.

Well, we didn't know what to do 'cause he jes' gives us some ole dull hoes an' axes to work wid. But we all went to work and as we cut down de trees and de poles, he tells us to build de fence 'round de field and we did. When we plants de co'n and de cotton, we jes' plant all de fence corners full, too. I nev'r seen so much stuff grow in all my born days. Several years [ears] of co'n to de stalk and dem big cotton stalks wuz a-layin' over de groun'. Some of de ole slaves dey say dey believe de Lawd knew sumpin' 'bout niggers, after all. He lets us put co'n in his crib. Den we builds cribs and didn't take long 'fore we could buy some hosses and some mules and some good hogs. Dem mangy hogs what our marster give us de first year wuz plum good hogs after we grease dem and scrub dem wid lye soap. He jes' give us de ones he thought wuz sho' to die, but we wuz a-gittin' goin' now and, 'fore long, we wuz a-buildin' better houses and feelin' kind of happy-like.

After Ole Marster dies, we keeps hearin' talk of Texas. Me an' my ole man — I's done been married several years den and had one little boy — well, we gits in our covered wagon wid our littles mules hitched to it and we comes to Texas. We worked as sharecroppers 'roun' Buffalo 'til my ole man he died. My boy wuz nearly grown den so he wants to come to San Angelo and work. So, here we is. He done been married long time now and got six chillun. Some of dem work at hotels and cafes and fillin' stations [gasoline stations] and in homes.

Huge bell used in Alabama to awaken slaves and to signal other activities

WILLIAM MATHEWS

Course I can 'lect [recollect] 'bout slavery. I is old and my eyesight am gone, but I can still 'lect. I ain't never forgit it.

My massa, old Buck Adams, could out-mean de debbil [devil] heself. He sho' hard, hard and sneaky as slippery ellum. Old Mary Adams, he wife, was 'most as hard as he was. Sometimes I used to wonder how deir chillen ever stood 'em.

Old Buck Adams brung my mammy and daddy from South Car'lina to work in de fields and my daddy's name was Economy Mathews and my mammy's name Phoebe. Simmons was her name 'fore she marry. I is born on old Buck's place, on December 25th in 1848. Dat plantation was in Franklin Parish, somewhere 'round Monroe in Louisiana.

Me and Bill Adams raised together. When he shoot a deer, I run home like greased lightin' and git de hoss [horse]. Sometimes he'd shoot a big hawg and I'd skin him.

When I got big 'nough, I'd drive deir carriage. I was what dey calls de "waiting boy". I sot in dat buggy and wait 'til dey come out of where dey was and den driv [driv pronouced like give] 'em off. I wasn't 'lowed to git out and visit 'round with de other slaves. No, suh, I had to set dere and wait.

De slaves git out in de fields 'fore sunup and work 'til black dark. Den dey come home and have to feel deir way in de house, with no light. My mammy and daddy field hands. My grandma was cook, and have to git in de cook pot 'bout four o'clock to git breakfas' by daylight. Dey et [ate] by candles or pine [knot] torches. One de black boys stand behin' 'em and hold it while dey et.

De clothes we wore was made out of dyed 'low's. Dat de stuff dey makes sackin' out of. Summertime us go barefoot but wintertime come, dey give you shoes with heels on 'em big as biscuits.

De quarters is back of de Big House and didn't have no floors. Dey sot plumb on de ground and build like a hawg [hog] pen. Dey cut down timber and stake it up at the corners and fill it in with timber with de bark on it. Dere was split log houses and round log houses and all sech like dat.

Dey have only fifty slaves on dat place, and it a big place, big 'nough for a hundred. But what dey do? Dey take de good slaves and sell 'em. Dat what dey do. Den dey makes de ones what am left do all de work. Sell, sell, all de time, and never buy nobody. Dat was dem.

Every Sat'day evenin', us go to de pitcher poke. Dat what dey calls it when dey issues de rations. You go to de smokehouse and dey weigh out some big, thick rounds of white pork meat and give it to you. De syrup weighed out. De meal weighed out. Dey never give us no sugar or coffee. You want coffee, you put de skillet on de fire and put meal in it and parch it 'til it 'most black, and put water on it. Mammy make salt water bread out of a li'l flour and salt and water.

Sometimes dey make de slaves go to church. De white folks sot up fine in deir carriage and drive up to de door and git de slaves out of one cabin, den git de slaves out of de nex' cabin, and keep it up 'til dey gits dem all. Den all de slaves walks in front of de carriage 'til dey gits to church. De slaves sot outside under de shade trees. If de preacher talk real loud, you can hear him out de window.

If a cullud man take de notion to preach, he couldn't preach 'bout de Gospel. Dey didn't 'low him to do dat. All he could preach 'bout was obey de massa, obey de overseer, obey dis, obey dat. Dey didn't make no passel of fuss 'bout prayin' den. Sometimes dey have prayin' meetin' in a cabin at night. Each one bring de pot and put deir head in it to keep de echoes from gittin' back [to the ears of the slaveowner. They couldn't let the slaveowner know that they were praying, but felt that they must pray aloud in order to be heard by God.] Den dey pray in de pot. Dat de Gawd's truth!

Like I done said, Massa sol' de good slaves in Monroe. Nobody marry in dem days. A gal go out and take a notion for some buck and dey make de 'greement to live together. Course, if a unhealthy buck take up with a portly [large] gal, de white folks sep'rate 'em. If a man a big, stout man, good breed, dey gives him four, five women.

Sometimes dey run 'way. It ain't done dem no good, for de dogs am put on dey trail. If you clumb de tree, dem dogs hold you dere 'til de white folks comes, and den dey let de dogs git you. Sometimes de dogs tore all dey clothes off, and dey ain't got nary a rag on 'em when dey git home. If dey run in de stream of water, de dogs gits after 'em and drowns 'em. Den Nick, de overseer, he whop [whipped] 'em. He drive down four stakes for de feets and hands and tie 'em up. Den he whop 'em from head to feets. De whip make out a hide, cut in strips, with holes punch in 'em. When dey hits de skin, it makes blisters.

All kind of war talk floatin' 'round 'fore de Yankees come. Some say de Yankees fight for freedom and some say dey'll kill all de slaves. Seems like it must have been in de middle of de war dat de Yankees come by. We hears somebody holler for us to come out one night and seed de place on fire. Time we git out dere, de Yankees gone. We fit [fought] de fire but we had to tote water in buckets. De fire burn up de gin house full of cotton and de cotton house, too, and de corn crib.

De Yankees allus come through at night and done what dey gwine to do, and den wait for more night 'fore dey go 'bout deir business. Only one time dey come in daylight, and some slaves jine [joined] dem and go to war.

All de talk 'bout freedom git so bad on de plantation, de massa make me put de men in a big wagon and drive 'em to Winfield. He say in Texas dere never be no freedom. I driv [driv pronounced like give] 'em fast 'til night and it take 'bout two days. But dey come back home. Massa say if he cotch [catch] any of 'em, he gwine shoot 'em. Dey hang 'round de woods and dodge 'round and 'round 'til de freedom man come by.

We went right on workin' after freedom. Old Buck Adams wouldn't let us go. It was way after freedom dat de freedom man [from the federal government] come and read de paper, and tell us not to work no more 'less us git pay for it. When he gone, old Mary Adams she come out. I 'lect what she say as if I jes' hear her say it. She say, "Ten years from today, I'll have you all back 'gain." Dat ten years been over a mighty long time and she ain't git us back yit, and she dead and gone.

Dey makes us git right off de place, jes' like you take a old hoss and turn it loose. Dat how us was. No money, no nothin'. I git a job workin' for a white man on he farm, but he couldn't pay much. He didn't have nothin'. He give me jes' 'nough to git a peck or two of meal and a li'l syrup.

I allus works in de fields and makes baskets, big old cotton baskets and bow baskets make out of white oak. I work down de oak to make de splits and makes de bow basket to tote de lunch. Den I make trays and mix [mixing] bowls. I go out and cut down de big poplar and bust off de big block and sit down straddle, and holler [hollow] it out big as I wants it, and made de bread tray. I make collars for hosses and ox whops and quirts out of beef hide. But I loses my eyesight a couple years back and I can't do nothin' no more. My gal takes care of me.

I come here [Texas] in 1931. Dat de first time I'm out of Franklin Parish [Louisiana]. I allus git along some way 'til I'm blind. My gal am good to me, but de days am passin' and soon I'll be gone, too.

The I WAS A SLAVE Book Collection
SUBTITLES OF BOOKS
EACH SUBTITLE IS <u>ONE SEPARATELY PUBLISHED</u> BOOK:

AVAILABLE NOW:
Book 1: Descriptions of Plantation Life
Book 2: The Lives of Slave Men
Book 3: The Lives of Slave Women
Book 4: The Breeding of Slaves
Book 5: The Lives of Slave Children

Upcoming Books — (being published in this order, one at a time*)

Book 6: Slave Auctions
Book 7: The Bullwhip and Other Treatments
Book 8: Runaways and Resistances
Book 9: Field and House Slaves
Book 10: How Plantations Operated
Book 11: Literacy and Unusual Circumstances
Book 12: Slaveowners: Hated and Loved
Book 13: Mulatto Slaves: Slave Mother and White Father
Book 14: City, Frontier, and Riverboat Slaves
Book 15: Slave Families and Separations
Book 16: Patrollers and the Ku Klux Klan
Book 17: The Lives of Slaveowners
Book 18: Remembering Africans and Indians
Book 19: Religion, Songs, and Communications
Book 20: The Civil War: What the Slaves Saw and Did
Book 21: Freedom!!!
Book 22: The Lives of Ex-Slaves: 1865-1937
Book 23: Plantation Days Remembered
Book 24: Superstitions, Ghost Stories, and Great Quotes

•••••••• **PLEASE NOTICE** ••••••••

At the time of the printing of this book, **only the first five books were available.** *Please do not order unpublished books in advance.*
<u>Please call 202-737-7827 to learn if additional books are available.</u>

(*When you order by mail, you are placed on our mailing list and will receive a postcard when each new book is published. There are no set publication times.)

ORDERING INFORMATION

Please look on page 63 for a list of available books.

PLEASE DO NOT ORDER BOOKS
THAT HAVE NOT BEEN PUBLISHED YET.

TO ORDER BY MAIL:
$9.50 for any one book
plus $8.50 for each additional book mailed at the same time
(Prices include postage and handling)

Example: Five books total $43.50

Mail your *printed* name and address with ZIP code,
(telephone numbers are optional, but should be included, just in case)
along with the **subtitles of each book** ordered,
quantities of each book, and your check or money order to:

American Legacy Books
P.O. Box 1393-B
Washington, DC 20013

To mail Discover, MasterCard, VISA, or American Express orders,
purchasers MUST include
(1) credit card number (2) expiration date,
(3) telephone number (a requirement), and (4) SIGNATURE.

Credit card orders by fax: 202-546-1919 must include **all** of above.

Current ordering information and publication dates
can be accessed on-line: **www.iwasaslave.com**
or call
202-737-7827
Automated information: 24 hours
Customer service: Monday-Friday, 9:00-5:00 Eastern time
for information and for placement of credit card orders

IMPORTANT: **At the time that this book was printed, only
1 through 5 were available.** Call to learn if more books have been
published: 202-737-7827 — OR — for a free brochure listing all
currently available books *(and price increases, if any, since this book
was published)*, please send a self-addressed and stamped envelope to
the above address.